Confessions of A Banger

Confessions of A Banger

JOHNNY BLAIR

authorHOUSE®

AuthorHouse™
1663 Liberty Drive
Bloomington, IN 47403
www.authorhouse.com
Phone: 1-800-839-8640

First published by AuthorHouse   10/07/2011

ISBN: 978-1-4670-2707-6 (sc)
ISBN: 978-1-4670-2708-3 (ebk)

Library of Congress Control Number: 2011918360

Printed in the United States of America

Any people depicted in stock imagery provided by Thinkstock are models, and such images are being used for illustrative purposes only.
Certain stock imagery © Thinkstock.

This book is printed on acid-free paper.

In the end, you think about the beginning.

When my mother wasn't paying attention I hit
the streets and I hit the streets real hard

I didn't know it was gonna get that deep
I didn't know it was get that thick

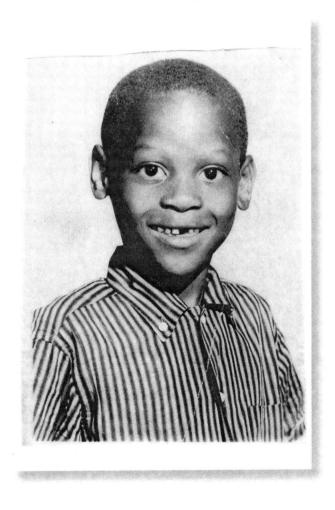

UNCENSORED AND UNCUT

THIS BOOK IS RAW

CHAPTER 1
THE YARD

THE YARD

We were on the yard in the lockup unit (the lock up unit is where they house the bad boys that cannot keep their hands and knives to themselves in the prison system.) talking about last night's game. I was called over to the fence that separated the two yards. I was told that a kite was coming over in code. Twenty minutes later they tossed the kite under the gate, and we fished it in. I took it to the side and decoded it. We talked and wrote in code to keep the guards from knowing what we talked about.

The kite said that we had a well known rat in our unit. We didn't know him because he was from another generation. They said he was a down dude at one time, but he got in over his head and turned junkie, started telling and giving up people to get from up under all that time.

A good place for a prideful rat to hide is amongst a generation of men who don't know him. Get these young and angry brothers fired up and have them do stuff he would never do. Tell a few war stories and share a few skills, gain their trust, and build up some walls of protection around him. That puts him in a position to mislead and then bad mouth the good brothers saying that they were dirty.

The letter was about Popcorn. He was also the trustee on our tier, and this was his fourth trip to the joint. I was not surprised. I didn't like the bastard anyway. Everything about him was shaky. He's the kind of Negro I couldn't stand, always skinning and grinning with and entertaining the cops. The brothers in the cell next to him late at night could hear the back slot of his cell open and conversations go on between Popcorn and the police. He was dirty.

If you sign up, you're gonna go out on missions. It is inevitable, and each cultural group has its own way of handling its business. Sometimes the stabbings or hits are one-on-one, and then there is teamwork. It saves time, energy, and a bloody mess.

I have seen them send three men to get one; two do the holding; and one do the stabbing. I have seen them send four to get one man. It was a large target; two did the holding and two did the stabbing. I saw two more on the sidelines ready to shortstop any interference or in case somebody tried to punk out, they got tagged.

Once I saw a seven-on-one the target that was large: 6'4' and about 350 pounds. Four were doing the holding and three doin' the hitting. It was like a pack of lions trying to take down an elephant—messy. The worst move I ever saw was nobody holding and all three had knives. They cut up their target but they also hospitalized each other.

Then you have the group discount package: the bastard you want has bodyguards around him at all times. You have to take the whole crew down in order to get that one bastard, and everybody gets blasted in the process. The more brutal and more vicious the attack and the more intimidating the stabbing, the clearer the message they send to the other prisoners: we are not to be fucked with.

I remember when I went on my first mission; I had to hit this dude. I was nervous as hell in the beginning. It was different from bangin'. I remember they told me when I finished with his ass, his heart better be hanging out of his chest or some throat meat better be on the ground and I'd better be splashing around kidney or liver fluids. This was how they talked to you.

I waited for a few more people to leave the television room and then I went in there on his ass. As I looked to the left and the right, I saw Sudan and a few others sitting in the seats drinking soda and eating chips, waiting on the show to start. I pulled the knife out of my coat and hit the dude's ass in the throat so he couldn't yell first. When he put his hands up to plead I ran his ass through again with the knife. He collapsed on the floor. I started to finish his ass off. I was drenched in blood, but in the back of my mind

I felt compassion. That proved to be a mistake because later on in life he became a fuckin' thorn in my side.

I walked out of the television room, got rid of the knife, and got out of the bloody clothes. They looked at me like I just hit a homerun to win the game. A celebration was taking place. Sudan said, "Excellent fuckin' job."

The alarm went off. Somebody had told the guards, and we were instructed to go to our cells. Dookie said to me, "Shit, you scared me. That was brutal." I love that shit

I lay on my bunk and ran it over in my mind a few times, After the first time it is nothing. I was eighteen then.

I waited for the last cell search to start cutting out a knife. At that point the guards were searching our cells at least once a week. Popcorn wouldn't come to the yard; he was scared that he might get his head cracked or throat cut, and he was right. Everything was ready but Popcorn still wouldn't come to the yard. We sent him zoos-zoos and some wams-wams, soups, and stamps.

He really didn't trust me. When I talked to him, he always stood back at least three steps from the bars and watched my hands at all times.

For three straight weeks we came to the yard strapped, hoping Popcorn would come out to the yard. I gave up hope so I made plans to burn him out of his cell or tag him with a pole.

The one day I left my blade in, he came to the yard because his homeboy was on our tier now. So we went on with our regular routine of running laps and exercising.

When we start running, Popcorn and his homeboy jumped in line and started running, too. Popcorn ran about ten laps and did a few exercises, and then he sat down. While he was still standing, I picked up a dumbbell and cracked him in his head. Blood shoots out of his head like a water fountain, and his homeboy screamed like a girl and ran. For about fifteen seconds there was mass confusion, and then the guards started shooting.

THE GUARDS DON'T STOP

The guards don't stop shooting until everybody is on the ground, stabbed or shot or not, clubbed or not. Then about twenty guards run onto the yard to secure it.

They grabbed me first slightly bruised I was searched for weapons and escorted off of the yard. The gurney came and got Popcorn. They threw him on top of the gurney. His ass won't be telling nothing any time soon; he was lucky they got me before I finished his ass off.

I spent about an hour in the infirmary and was taken to the isolation cells. I was already in the lockdown unit; what else could they do?

I was sitting on the bed in my cell reading when the guard passing out tonight's mail place this manila envelope on my cell bars. It was a diagnostic evaluation report done on me. It was a four-page letter explaining how I became the way I am. I found the report disturbing and way off base. I was angry because they blamed everyone but me for my failures and violent behavior. I don't blame anyone but myself for my dumb and shameful and disgraceful behavior.

The door was always open for me to walk through and step away. I got lost in it, but it did not start when I was fourteen, like they stated in the report. It began when I was a child. Everything I let in, every door I opened, and every road I went down brought me closer to the next one and my eventual fate.

That quiet kid that used to smile, laugh, and joke and just wanted to run and play ball left a long time ago. It may be hard to believe but there was a time when we all were kids, just kids. I went to school every day, loved baseball and football, and had goals and dreams. I was five years old when I saw my first gang fight in the projects. I saw about 20 little boys ranging from the age of 8 to13 running back to their side of the projects. Thirty seconds later here comes the brothers from the other side of the projects pursuing them. This kid with the pompadour hair do and rag around his head in the first group yells something. and the first group stops dead in their tracks and make a u—turn and start running toward the first group.Both groups clash in the middle of the street.It sounded like a violent car crash when the two groups clashed into each other. Both sides were gladiating real hard in the middle of the street for a while the battle was even. Then the dude with pompadour hair do broke out with this chain.Every time he would hit somebody with that chain they would yell and fall and retreat. They beat them down and ran them back to their side of the projects.Then the dude with the pompadour hair-do step into the middle of the street and through his arms in the air screamed like a mad man. and something jumped in my heart.

NICKERSON GARDENS & THE SOUTH

As far back as I can remember I can't remember living any other place but Nickerson Gardens. Some people were ashamed to say that they lived in the projects. I accepted who I was and what I was early in life. I didn't have that hang-up about being ashamed of where I was from or wanting to be something else other than what I was. I love who I am and I know who I am.

The Watts area was a predominately southern community, especially from Texas and Louisiana, when I was growing up in it.

In kindergarten Roy and I were the only kids in our class born in Los Angeles; everybody else was from Texas and Louisiana and other parts of the South, and a few from the East. You could see it in their walk and hear it in their talk; each Southern family brought with them some of the South—the different foods, the clothes, the customs, the stories, the music, and the cooking. Also the fears and hang-ups they had to face in the South.

When I was growing up, brothers had names, like Dove, Sonny Boy, Donald Ray, Jimmy Lee, Willie B., Garland., George Washington Smith and Abraham Lincoln Johnson, and names from the Bible. They had nicknames, like Bay Ronny, Hocks, Skillet, Cornbread, Patches, Buttons, Bus, and Truck.

The girls had names, like Spring, Phyala, Yasmin, Timmie Lee, Georgia and nicknames like: Bacon, Kitty, Peaches, and Cookie.

That was a really special time period in the history of America; there was still a kind of innocence. There was censorship and strictness in every element of society. There were things you just couldn't say or do. I grew up in a time when the world was black and white. For us as a people, there was a tremendous amount of respect shown toward each other and for each other.

It was a common occurrence to see little girls on their porch playing with dolls or see them playing jacks or playing jump rope or playing hopscotch in front of the house, and to see little boys in the parking lot playing baseball. Life was real simple and basic, fun was right outside your front door.

There was a different kind of mother and father raising their children. There was structure and order in the black family. Many men took their places as the head of the family; some didn't. Men headed the coming together, taking care of, and preserving the family bond. You knew your place as a child, and you knew to stay in it. In the families where there was no father the grandfather or the uncles stepped in and filled the gap. It wasn't easy raising kids in the projects.

My Mother

My mother was from a small town in Texas. She came to California when she was twenty-one years old to escape the racism in the South and for a shot at opportunity. The small town she was from was a farm town. When you finished school, you either farmed, picked cotton or worked for the railroad or for the local factory or mill. None of them were really hiring women. Those that had the heart and mind went on to college.

My father was one of them Texas slickers that preyed on country girls new in the big city. My aunt said he was a charmer. We were lucky if we saw him once a year. Our only ties to that side of the family were my aunt and my grandmother.

My grandmother was the kind of woman that would send food to families having a hard time. If she couldn't get anyone to bring her to Los Angeles to pick me up, she would ride on a bus from Pasadena to the projects in Watts to pick me up to spend time with her. I understood that she loved me. My grandmother lost her battle with cancer when I was six.

My mother was one of those women whose expressions never changed. It was hard to tell if she was going through something or not. I am sure that there were difficult times.

I never felt anything but love from my mother except when I crossed the line.

My grandfather was my hero, my role model. I admired his strength, courage and wisdom and his love for his family. He told me when I was about seven years old that after God comes family and the family was the first unit God created. He went on to say you are nothing without God and family; life is nothing without God and family.

What our grandparents and aunts and uncles passed on to us was the importance of family and preserving the family bond. That was the purpose of the family gatherings, the picnics, parties celebrating birthdays, coming together to watch the championships; all done to bring us together as a family and to keep the family circle tight. At that time no one in our family went without or sat in the dark, and there were always presents under the Christmas tree. I thank God for family.

Home was a loved-filled place with Mama. God bless Mama for all she did for us.

THE HOOD

In the projects you started everything early: fighting, stealing, lying, cheating, standing up for yourself, and standing together.

Nickerson Gardens was one of those places that seemed to manufacture bullies. As soon as we were allowed to play outside unsupervised, the thugs were all on us. They took my brother's bike he had just got for Christmas and kicked his ass. My uncle gave my older brother a baseball bat and made him go back with my cousin, and told them they'd better not come back home without the bike. They came back later on that night all lumped up; one with his teeth loosened up and no bike. They got cleaned up and went to bed.

The brothas that took my brother's bike weren't bullies; they were villains. It was that Popeye and his brother Deadeye. They both looked like they were homeless, and they both smelled like fresh piss every morning. Popeye's eyes rotated when he talked to you, so you didn't know if he was talking to you or the person standing next to you. Most of the time he didn't have to say anything at all; it was all in his eyes and his voice that made kids give that money up.

When he did talk, he liked to take his finger and stick it in your forehead. They extorted other kids out of money, clothes, shoes, and bikes. You had to be on your toes whenever Popeye and his brother Deadeye were around, because if you fought one you had to fight the other. Some of the kids would see them coming and go back in the house. If Deadeye was talking to you, you wanted to make sure you were standing back at least two or three feet because he would wet you up. He had a leaky faucet. Whatever Popeye said, Deadeye would confirm it with water.

I have seen them make other kids get down and kiss their shoes; make other kids go in the store and steal for them; shoot kids with BB guns; and the worst crime I heard they committed was when Popeye made these two kids at our school lay on their stomach, and he stood over them and peed on both of them.

It was a waste of time to talk to their mother about the stuff they were doin.' She didn't care. If she wasn't drunk, she was on her way to the liquor store to get drunk.

Popeye and Deadeye and two of their friends jumped my brother one day when he was coming back from the store for my mother. I ran down the street to help my brother, and I hit Deadeye as hard as I could behind his ear. He jumped up, yelled, and grabbed his head, but I didn't see Popeye. He caught me with a right cross between the eyes and right on the nose. He sat me on my ass. Popeye was getting ready to step to me and finish me off. Then I heard a boom.

Deadeye yelled "Drop and run." Then I heard another boom and saw Popeye laid out on the ground with blood coming from his head. I saw Angel standing over us with a baseball bat asking if we were alright, and then I got up and said, "I'm glad you're my friend."

I went into the house and looked in the mirror. I had my first shiner. My mother told me I'd better learn to duck.

From the beginning Angel exhibited this aggressive personality, and it was clear that he was running the show. He wasn't for no shit. They didn't ask me shit. They told me to be there and you knew that if you didn't show up, that was your ass.

If you didn't stand up for yourself or hold your ground, they would stampede all over you and some of them were merciless. So it was fight back, take that ass-whippin' or stay in the house.

TIME

We were really blessed to grow up in a time when black people really stuck and stood together. We showed each other so much respect. Family helped family; friends helped friends; and neighbors helped neighbors. That is, before all of the anger, the treachery, the jealousy, the drive-bys, and the crack.

It was a different kind of parents raising children.

It was a different kind of teachers teaching the children.

A different kind of preacher preaching the Word of God

A different kind of leader leading our community

A different kind of rhythm flowing through the black community A different kind of love

ANGEL

The very first kid I can ever remember meeting in my life was

Anthony Thomas. His mother called him Angel, so we called him

Angel. To us he was known as Angel, but to the other kids in school and in our neighborhood he was known as that little bad ass black motha-fucka or that little busy black bastard. He was special. Angel and his mother moved out here from Texas when he was about three years old.

Even when I was a kid, the hood was territorial. There were street gangs. The brothas that lived by the gym field called themselves the wolf pack. They were known to jump on anybody they caught out of bounds or on their side.

Angel, Li'l Bobby, and Roy were on their side acting up, taking money from other kids. They were confronted by two members of the pack, and they beat the shit out of the two members of the pack.

An hour later five members of the pack came on our side looking for Angel. We sent them home all lumped up.

A few days later while I was having dinner, the Pack swooped on us about twenty of them. They had Angel, Roy, Bobby, Al, and Mumbles surrounded completely. They had rakes, sticks, torn pieces of water hoses; this was well planned, and they moved in on them and beat the shit out of them. Witnesses say that they had Angel pinned down holding his legs and arms while Fat Mike sat in his chest and teed off on him.

Fat Mike said, "I am tired of you, you little black bastard. What'd I tell you about fucking around?"

They beat Angel all in his face, stomped him in his nuts, and dragged him around by his hair. Fat Mike kicked Angel is his side and they ran. They fought back hard but there were too many of them.

My oldest brother sat in the window and watched the whole thing go down. Because he didn't like Angel he didn't say anything to me. I asked my mother if I could please be excused from the dinner table. I grabbed my baseball and I ran outside, but by the time I had got there the pack was gone.

I had to rally the troops; we had been invaded. I went over there to do a casualty check. Angel had a mouse under both his eyes and was still laying on the ground trying to massage the pain out of them nuts. Roy and Corn had welts on both arms from trying to block the sticks and water hose.

While I was giving my motivational speech, Mumbles came back with a bunch of sticks. I told them, "Get up. Let's go get them bastards."

There were twelve of us. They took the long way home. We cut threw Parmalee and ran hard. We came up behind them; they were out of breath and must have dropped their sticks along the way. We flanked them from the rear. Their eyes got as big ass baseballs when they turned around and saw us. There was nowhere to go, no path of escape. We moved in and beat them like they stole something. There was blood on the wall when we finished; and they had knots on their heads.

I surprised myself. Angel told the others to hold Fat Mike down. Angel walked over to him and kicked him in his face. Fat Mike was wobbling, and Angel sat in his chest and went to work. We had to pull Angel off of him.

This lady came outside and threatened to call the police, and we victoriously trotted home. Two days later Fat Mike sent word that he wanted to fight Angel one-on-one at a mutual spot. Fat Mike didn't know what he had just signed up for.

Mr. Johnson was a retired custodian that opened up his garage and turned into a boxing facility for the young kids that wanted to box. His best student was Anthony Thomas. Angel spent more time in that garage on the bags than he did at home. When Angel finished with Fat Mike, he had knots all over his face.

Fat Mike wasn't done. We were invited to this party on their side; they saw us in the party and went got everybody they could find there were five of us and about thirty of them. They attacked us inside the party tearing up this lady's good dam furniture. There were too many of them. I was getting hit from all directions. I was throwing lefts and rights backing my way to the door. We were all outside except Angel; he was in there still slugging it out. The men broke it up and made us all go home our separate ways.

The final conflict: we issued a challenge. We told them to meet us at Verbum Dei Friday evening. Fat Mike recruited Hocks and his street gang and a bunch of other kids. We got there first and waited for them. There were fifteen of us.

They showed up 30 minutes later when they hit the gate and hopped the fence. It looked like there were about 100, but there were only 60 of them. I knew that all of us would fight to the end. The enemy brought a lot of supporters and spectators with them.

Depending on who was winning would determine if they remained spectators or not.

Angel stepped out front and said half them boys over there still wet the bed and still sucked their thumbs and needed their mothers to tuck them in at night. I refused to lose to some bed-wetting pee—pee boys. If we charged them bastards real hard and put it on them, I bet half of them would break and run.

Angel ain't never been all there; he charged them by his self yelling something, and we took off behind him. He made them break rank and when they saw us they panicked; half on them took off and squeezed threw a little hole in a gate. We beat the shit out of the rest. Fat Mike we stomped his fat ass. I learned a valuable lesson that day: size is nothing; numbers don't mean a thing. Angel was a great motivator. He brought the best out in all of us. This last sentence is for my boy Eugene Radcliff who always showed up regardless of the odds he passed away at a very young age.Rest in peace homie

Angel didn't change; he got worse. He became General Angel, who would have kids fire on other kids to prove their loyalty to him. He told Paul, "Go over and fire up Teddy, and when you hit him I better feel it way over here, or Teddy better be getting up off of the ground or I am fucking you up."

Angel started going in and out of jail on small stuff, and then bigger stuff. Each time he came home he would be worse than before. Whenever he got out he knew where to find me: at the school, playing ball.

ANGEL 2

A lot of people didn't understand how Angel became the way he was. In the beginning he was the kind of kid that smiled all of the time, was always in a good mood, and was a lot of fun to be around. When his mother changed, his whole life changed. Mrs. Mabel was a sweet country girl when she came to California, but she got in with the wrong people, got hooked on drugs and alcohol, and her life took a drastic change. Sometimes after school we went to the candy store and on our way home we would pass the liquor store; Angel's mom would be standing behind the store with the winos drinking and talking loud. Sometimes they fondled his mother as we passed by. She would speak to Angel, and he would walk right by her like he didn't know her. He was very, very embarrassed by her behavior.

Sometimes she would stagger home real late at night, and sometimes she didn't come home at all. She would get into the cars of strangers and turn tricks, and sometimes she would bring strangers home and turn tricks. Some of the tricks would refuse to pay her and beat her. In the process of coming to his mama's aid, Angel would get beat up.

Mrs. Mabel didn't cook or clean or do laundry. If not for his grandmother who lived on the other side of the projects and neighbors, he would not have eaten nor had clean clothes to wear to school.

That was my boy. What I had, he had. When I ate, he ate. Angel would knock on my window late at night and ask me to help me look for his mother. I would grab my baseball bat and jump out of the window. Sometimes we would find her passed out behind the liquor store. One time the winos were running a train on her as we walked up on them. Angel asked me for the bat, and he clubbed the shit out of the one on top of his mother and hit the other ones as they tried to run. I don't know how we did it but we got her dressed and got her home. He loved his mother but he couldn't stand the way she was.

Around October of that year Angel and I competed in the kick, punt, and pass contest. I came in first, and Angel came in third. We rushed home to show our mothers the ribbons we won. We stopped at his house first. He went upstairs to show his mother, and he found her with a needle stuck in her arm. She wasn't dead, but it took the ambulance two hours to get there. She passed away somewhere along the way.

I didn't sleep at all that night. I waited for him, and I was told the next day that she had passed away.

Angel had to go live on the other side with his grandmother. I didn't get a chance to see him until the day of the funeral. It was a closed casket funeral. Angel became a different person after the passing away of his mother. He became quiet, distant, and merciless. He bullied the bullies. Then he started going to jail for short periods of time, and then long periods of time. Whenever he got out, I was always the first person he looked up, and I was just as glad to see him. He knew he could always find me playing ball somewhere.

ANGEL 3

He was the kind of kid that had an extremely high amount of confidence and he inspired us to push to do things on the next level. He couldn't stand cry babies. I remember once Dead Eye and Pop jumped on Roy, and Roy walked home with tears coming from his eyes.

Angel walked up to Roy and socked him in his stomach and said, "Stop that fuckin' crying, acting like a little punk." Roy dropped to his knees from the punch, and while he was down Angel socked him in the back and said, "Dry it up. Let's go get them bastards."

We caught them strong-arming two other kids and we laid them out.

CHAPTER 2
THE EARLY YEARS

MY HOMIES

There were still a few Italian families living in the homes outside of the projects. Their families still owned some of the local businesses.The Italians kids didn't go to school with us but we would meet up at the school and play ball with us on the weekends.After the Watts riot they were all gone.

Some of the families like the Wade's. Tarkingtons, Shermans, Trayons, Sheppards, Hamiltons, Morgans, Williams, and Henderson families have been in the bricks just as long as we have. The Carters came later, along with Jefferey P. and Jefferey K. The best ball players, Wade, Mark J., Erick, Stevie H., and Leonard W., Waylon were all in our area. They won championships for our school and beat the champs in other areas. We took it as an honor whenever they asked us to play with them. This was where we got our game.

My baseball partners were Keith and Kenneth Henderson, Darryl Johnson and Adell, Thomas Lindsey, Ernest Rhodes and Rickey S and my brother George. We would play anybody that showed up, and win. We came from that generation that had to learn to make do or be creative with what we had. Most of the gloves and bats that were given or donated to us were throwaways by people who cared. We had two Louisville Slugger bats that were broken in two. We drove three nails through one of them and drilled the holes in the other one and taped them both up. The gloves all needed a quick mending job.

Each of us had the name and the number of his favorite baseball player on the back of his shirt somewhere. There were a lot of 24s, 21s, 44s, Aaron, Mays, Clemente, Santos, Stargell, the Davis boys, Brooks, and Frank Robinson. The boys that pitched wore Koufax, Drysdale, Marichal, and Gibson on back of their shirts. We tried to walk like them, dig into the batter's box like them, run like them, catch like them, and bat like them. Baseball was big when we were growing up. Then we would go home and listen to the Dodgers on the radio.Life was real simple

BASEBALL

We were in the parking lot playing catch with the baseball when this gigantic figure of a kid stepped over to us and said, "This is how you do it, young blood." It was the dude with the pompadour hairdo and the chain that screamed like a wild man.

Angel told me, "Don't let go of that bat. We might have to take his big crazy down. His ass ain't all there."

I gave him my glove, and he introduced himself to us. He told us his name was B.B. Washington. He talked to us and played catch with us for a long time. B.B. played catch with us all that summer, and then he disappeared. The kids in the neighborhood said he was in jail.

112TH STREET SCHOOL

The school system was very different at that time. The teaching methods were different and what we were taught was different. God was honored and given the respect due Him. They were very strict about what went on in a classroom. Some of the things that just weren't tolerated: talking back, cussing, fighting, ditching school.

Discipline was allowed in the school system then, and that meant you could get snatched up by the seat of your pants or the back of your shirt. It was nothing like having to take swats or getting your knuckles popped. The girls got paddled, too, and got their knuckles popped. It was all done to keep control of the students and create an environment for learning. Because of all the things that were going on at the time, certain things had to be programmed into us.

It was in the second grade on the steps of 112th Street School that we established the bond; there was a blood ceremony and an oath.

Our relationship with our teachers was very close in the 1960s. I want to thank my teachers at 112th Street School for going beyond job duties and preparing us for the time we lived in, beginning with Mrs. Sterling, Mrs. Chavis, Mrs. Stoval, Mrs. Tolbert, Mrs. Anthony, Mrs. Frankie Johnson, Mr. White, Mr. Wayand, Mr. Beaver, and a special thanks to Mr. Mansfield. Also special to us were the custodians, Big Bubba and Mr. Jones. The lady that made our summers was Mrs. Pridget.

I wouldn't trade my childhood for anything. I had a ball growing up in the projects in Watts.

THE CHURCH 2

Growing up in the 1960s the church had a multi-functional role. It was the place where we were taught about God and the

Word of God. It was also a place where ministries helped struggling families, the homeless, and made guidance available.

During the Civil Rights Movement, the church served as headquarters for the movement. It was the center of all of the activities—the meetings and the organizing of marches and protests—in our communities.

It was December, and the pastor of the local church and other members were in the community handing out leaflets that invited anyone and everybody to come see the Christmas play. My mother made us go; most of our street was there.

There is something about December that touches the hearts of men and women and puts them in the spirit to give and help. The young lady that was the host of the program walked up to the mike and spoke about the real reason for the season and walked off. Then this little boy walked onto the stage and grabbed the mike and began to sing "Away in a Manger."

I was shocked because it was Roy. I didn't know he had that kind of talent. He got the loudest ovation that night. Angel and I were surprised, because Roy could out-cuss most men; breaking into houses was his other hobby. After that performance in church, we would get together at night, form a circle, and Roy would give us our parts and we would sing.

When Roy wasn't singing, he and TD were breaking into houses. TD stood for tooth decay. TD would boost Roy into the window and once Roy was inside he would open the door and let TD in. They got busted two weeks later and were sent to Juvi, but they both escaped and were on the run.

Roy found me at school and told me he would be at the hideout until he figured out his next move. I was sneaking

Roy food from my house to the hideout. That went on for about a week until some old lady told on him, and he was recaptured and taken back to Juvenile Hall.

Mama

My mother used to whip real hard and energetically when I was a kid. Whatever she could find to whip you with is whatever you got beat with. The belt, shoe, pot, broken chair leg, or mop. One time she got me with a box of cornflakes. Her favorite weapon was the extension cord. When she couldn't find anything to beat you with, she would start throwing jabs and right hooks.

For my oldest brother, all that my mother had to do was to show him the extension cord and he would start crying. I could hear him in the other room. x okay I'll tell, I'll tell it was Johnny. When she did whoop him, she would have to barricade the house first, because he would break for the streets. He would do this thing where he would lay on the ground and act like he had passed out. My mother would kick his ass back to life.

My other brother said that if she was gonna beat his ass, she'd better put on her track shoes because she was gonna have to get his ass on the run. He would hop around like a damn rabbit; he wore her out.

Most of the time it was just me and her and the extension cord. Me, I could take an ass whopping. I would weigh the crime and the punishment. Do it and come home and take the ass-whopping; it only hurt for a while. When I wouldn't cry, it made her mad, and she would whoop me harder and I still wouldn't cry. I knew I had a high tolerance for pain.

My Brothers

My oldest brother thought it was his rightful place to assume command of the household whenever my mother went out at night. Whatever he said we were supposed to hop to it and get it done without question. I would tell him, "Don't ask me to do shit because I am not gonna do it." He would reply "Don't have me fuck you up." He knew I would fight him back or pick up something and use it. His friends would tell him "I wouldn't take that shit off of my little brother. I'd kick his little ass until he got the message." He had a bad habit of telling on me, so I took a lot of ass-whoopings because of snitching. I was in the house on punishment because of his telling.

My oldest brother liked to make chocolate milk and put it in the freezer and let it chill, and go outside and then come back in and drink it. One day I took a box of Ex-Lax and put the whole thing in his chocolate and stirred it up until it dissolved, and then I put his drink back in the freezer. When he came in the house to use the bathroom, I took his key from the table. I snatched it so he couldn't get back in the house. He came out of the bathroom, drank his milk, and went back inside.

I sat in the window and watched him play across the street and then I saw him grab his stomach and frown up. He ran home and knocked on the door, but I didn't answer. He said, "You little bastard, I know you are in there. Open the door." Then he started doin' the I-got-to-shit dance and knocked on the neighbor's door, but they weren't at home, either. Then he started doing the I-got-to-really-shit dance and took off for the school, but it was too late. Cream of shit everywhere came running down the side of his leg. He stayed mad at me a long time for that one. I had to walk around armed with a bat for about two damn weeks, but that broke up the telling.

JUST A POOR BOY FROM WATTS

One time we were on Central, and this white man was down on all four doing cement work. He was in field goal range, and I couldn't pass up a field goal. I took four steps back and two steps to the right. I ran up and I got all of my foot in his ass. I could see the shoeprint. He skid head first across six feet of cement with his arms extended like Superman. He took his time and got up with wet cement all over him, called me a name, and the chase was on. He made the mistake of following us into the projects. The brothers at the dice game tossed his ass.

The same spot the following week, a white man was painting a building. He was about eight feet in the air on a ladder before I kicked it out from under him. He chased us for a minute but he had enough sense not to come into the projects. He flagged the police down and the chase was on. We climbed up in a tree, hid while below they walked by us about three times, calling us all kinds of niggas. (I am talking about the police.)

THE PLAYGROUND

Our elementary school was turned into a playground during the summer. It was open for play. We were there every day, Monday through Friday, playing ball, caroms, games, and other activities. We also represented our school in sports events competing against other schools. They had this big track meet at our school, and the top two finishers in each event got to go to the Junior Olympics.

I won the 50-yard dash and the 440-yard dash. For two weeks Mr. White worked with us on our events and finally that time arrived. We got on the bus and we rode over to the old Pepperdine University to compete. Kids had come from all over to run in this track meet. Many of kids were running in professional uniforms, but I have on cut-off jeans, a Dodgers shirt, and my PF flyers.

My first event was the 50-yard dash. The top two finishers in each heat went to the finals. I slipped on my start and went on to barely win. Thirty minutes later in the finals, I was placed in the middle of the field, and when the starter's gun went off, I came out blastin'. So did the kid next to me. At one point he was slightly ahead but I got him at the end. I got a pep talk from Russell, and I was encouraged by my friends to win.

As I approached the starting line, I heard the voices of Denise Coleman, Yasmin Anderson, and Keith Henderson saying, "Go Johnny! Go Johnny!"

In the 440, they lined up twelve kids. When the gun went off, they came out running like it was the 100-yard dash. I just paced myself. By the 200-yard mark, most of them had faded. I had three kids in front of me when we hit the 300-yard mark. I gave it all I had. I ran them down and won. At that time they didn't give out medals; they gave out only red, white and blue ribbons. I was proud representing my school and Watts. God bless you Mr. White and God bless you Mrs. Pridgette and Russell.

In the late 1960s I began to see a change in my family. Uncle Sam began calling the men, and some of them began going away for long periods at a time to jail. There was a big rise in the use of drugs and alcohol. My girl cousins were called to motherhood early.

Then everybody began moving further away. The only time we saw each other was at weddings and funerals. There were less family gatherings. Everything seemed to be slipping away.

THE WATTS RIOT

I don't know how it started, but I know I wasn't allowed to go outside because of what was going on. I could see smoke coming from all directions of Los Angeles. Whatever was going on was being televised on local and national television. I could see people running down the street with food, clothes, furniture, and appliances. They would drop the stuff off at home and go back out to loot some more. You could see the National Guard riding through the streets heavily armed.

That is my memory of the Watts riot.

FOOTBALL

Our football games in the projects were brutal, revengeful, and sometimes bloody. I was under the impression that the object of the game was to see who could send the most people home limping or to the hospital. There were no rules; anything went: clipping, dragging you down by the groin, sticking their fingers in your eyes, grabbing you by them damn naps, elbowing you to the head, getting you in a headlock, and riding you like a steer.

It was our job to punish you for running or catching the ball. We would hold you up and wouldn't let you fall so everybody could get a piece of you. We would travel and play other streets and neighborhoods. It was always some shit in the game when we played other streets in the projects: two quarters of fighting and two quarters of football.

One time I tried to tackle Rhea Boyce. I grabbed him around the legs, and he dragged me about ten feet and walked into the end zone for touchdown. I felt like I had been hit by a train.

Most of us that lived in the general area were taught to play the game of football by Big Will Henderson who took the time. We all wanted to be able to run like Greg Coleman to fly.

Tyrone Bone

Everybody had somebody locally that they admired and looked up to. For us, it was Tyrone Bone. We watched and studied him. We imitated and tried to do everything we saw him do; we walked like him, ran like him, talked like him, and he did it all so effortlessly.

He wore gators and high top biscuits and he had them in every color to match his suits. The women were in awe of him. They would come outside watering the grass or doing yard work, hoping that he would notice.

What stuck with me more than anything else he did was the way he would look out after the friends he grew up with. He gave the girls money for groceries and for toys at Christmas. Now, that's a friend.

He came out here when he was four years old with his mother from the South with absolutely nothing. They didn't even have a place to stay. Thank God she ran into this elderly black woman who took them in and watched Tyrone while she worked.

Six months later they moved into Nickerson Gardens. He began hustling at an early age. His specialty was gambling and the numbers. He got A's in math because of his ability to remember and juggle numbers. His hustle was so strong that he moved him and his mama out of the projects before he entered high school. He would always come back and visit and encourage us to stay in school and do something with our life.

He would encourage us all to be different, and he would always give us a math problem to solve in our head. If we answered it correctly he gave us a dollar. The jealous brothers talked about him behind his back but they didn't want any part of him. Tyrone loved to fight.

EZ AND EZRA

Two new kids moved on our block; the eldest kid's name was Ezekiel, called Ez, and the youngest Ezra. Ez played baseball which made it easy to fit in. Ezra was on crutches and wore polio braces. We would meet at 112th Street School; divide ourselves into teams; toss the bat and play. We played like it was the World Series; we played hard.

We would break about noon and go to the alleys and streets in search of bottles. At that time in Watts you could take bottles to the store and get money for them. As a group we would find about thirty bottles and get two, three, and five cents for the bottles. Back then sodas were ten or thirteen cents, chips five cents, and cookies a nickel we bought it all. With the leftover money we would buy penny candy. We start playing ball again and play until we couldn't see.

About the fall of 1965, Ezra's health took a turn for the worse, and we saw less and less of him. He was confined to his bed. His mother, Mrs. Janet, for some reason, decided to throw him a birthday party the next day. We didn't have time to get him anything. We took an old baseball, and we all signed our names on it. Mrs. Janet let us all go up and sing happy birthday to him and present him with our present. When we got to his room, he was so surprised. It was hard for Roy and the others to hold back the tears. Ezra had dwindled down to nothing. He loved that baseball.

Two weeks later Ezra passed away. A hundred and fifty people squeezed into a small local church. At the end of the service, as I looked onto his casket, he laid there in peace. When I saw the baseball we all autographed in his hand, it made me smile.

Night

When I was kid I would sit in the window and watch them do their thing in the projects or get loose. There was never a dull moment in the projects; somebody was always getting cussed out, fighting, doing transactions, playing dice games and card games, and winos and drug addicts were acting out and acting up, stealing, outsiders getting jumped. The women had it like a soap opera in the projects lying, spreading rumors, and the next thing you knew they were rolling around in the grass pulling out each other's hair.

At night time the vampires came out. That was when the projects turned into something different and dangerous. The thugs, wheelers and dealers, stuff talkers, and crooks all took their spot.

CHAPTER 3
MARKHAM

MARKHAM JUNIOR HIGH

I was very excited about the first day of school; so excited I hardly slept the night before. When I arrived at school that first day, it was all I had thought it would be. When I stepped onto campus for that very first time, I knew it was gonna be special.

We were all sitting in our chairs waiting for our homeroom teacher to arrive. In walked this dude that looked like he just came back from Woodstock. He hit us with a peace sign and wrote his name on the board. His first talk was about our responsibilities now that we were in junior high school. He told us in so many words that the baby years were over.

I wasn't too crazy about having to strip for P.E., and this going from class to class thing and having to keep track of homework and notes was a little hectic in the beginning, but you get used to it.

I was fascinated also with all of the beautiful girls that were there. The transition from cowboys to girls was a little slow. If one of them would have said something to me, I probably would have turned about four or five different colors.

MARKHAM 1-A

On the first day of school, it took me a few minutes find my homeroom. The very first kid I met in my homeroom was Diamond David Johnson who sat right behind me. DJ had on some real colorful bell bottoms and some All Stars. That day I also met

Eddie Tunstall, Larry Downs, Hubert Richardson, Billy Jefferson, Keith and Reggie Brown, Anthony Brackins, Anthony Boman, Curtis Andrews, Garry Mayes, James Wimberly, Jessie Powell; and young ladies named Essetta Barns, Debra Tillman, Tanya Dinwiddie, and Debra Tate. Also with me there from my elementary school were Keith Adkins, Denise Coleman, Yvonne, Connie, Vonetta, so I wasn't alone.

I used to see DJ in the projects riding around on mini-bikes and motor cars. What I didn't know at the time was that he did all of the work on them himself. He was very talented and smart. I don't think he went to school; his brothers didn't. Later on I found out he liked stealing cars. This was how I learned to drive. Markham gave us the opportunity to meet the brothers and the sisters on the other side of Watts.

What was special about Markham at that time was the sports program. We played each sport representing our homeroom, and teams were coached by our homeroom teachers. This homeroom sports program kept a lot of kids off the streets and out of trouble. It also established a unique relationship between students and teachers because of the time spent together.

The marquee was the school dance held after school on Fridays. I wasn't gonna go but they talked me into it. They didn't know I was that bashful. The dance was packed with girls of all kinds. About five or six songs were played before I decided that I needed to grab a girl and hit the dance floor. I was on the sidelines building myself up to go over there to ask a girl to dance. I waited for the right song to come on. I walked over there with the boys and did it. I asked a girl that was in one of my classes to dance.

MARKHAM 3

Around the time I was in the 8th grade was when the Green Jackets Gang came out. They could easily be spotted; they all wore green jackets. They didn't kick up a lot of dust but you knew they were there. One day they were all lined up and down Compton Avenue taking lunch money. There were probably thirty to forty members. I think I was more impressed with the brotha that led them. There were two big names that stood out at Markham and Gompers, and both were from Nickerson Gardens: Rhea and Tyvee. One a gifted gymnast and the other, next to Rickey Bell, the best football player I ever saw in our time. From the shoulders they were the baddest dudes at those schools.

After Ezra moved away, Carl Steward moved in. His parents split up. Carl's dad was a pimp and so was his grandfather and great grandfather. Everything his dad was instilling in Carl was a young pimp in training. Carl just wanted to be regular kid, go to school, and play ball. When you heard something over and over you began to believe it. The real mistake came when the mother sent Carl to live with father that summer.

He came back that September a different person. He didn't play ball anymore and he didn't hang with us. He said it wasn't profitable. Whenever girls passed by, Carl would jump into what we call a pimp stance. He stayed sharp and was always in the mirror. He was real cool. He had one voice for us and another voice for the girls. We found out he was charging the big girls and the girls considered unattractive for his time. He had them all stealing money from their mothers and fathers. He told this one young lady, "If you really love me, go get me $200," and she did. When her mother found the money missing, she beat her stupid ass and made her take her to Carl's house. It got nasty. The police got involved. When all was said and done,

Carl had to give the money back, and his mother sent him to live with his dad.

About a week later my brother was coming home from school when he was jammed up by crazy Larry across the street from where we lived. Larry called him names. My brother tried to walk away but when he did, Larry socked him in the back of his head. My brother got up and tried to pick up his school books. He started to head for home. My mother was standing across the porch watching it all. She came across the street and made my brother fight him. He dropped my brother three times and beat him from one end of the street to another. I wanted to help but my mother wouldn't let me. One day his ass would be mine.

PREACHER

When Carl moved away, Joe Hunter moved in when his parents separated. Joe was skeptical about playing with us because in the beginning he had heard that we were some unsaved heathens. He was a preacher's son that didn't want to be corrupted. In the beginning he wouldn't leave the porch and every other word that came out of his mouth was Jesus this and Jesus that. He could quote scriptures and tell you what they meant. So we began to call him Preacher.

The first time he got a real taste of the projects was when he went to the ice cream truck to buy ice cream, and Michael Swan asked him for his money. Preacher went into this explanation on how it was wrong to take from other people. The next thing Preacher knew was he was on his back on the ground looking up and seeing stars. Michael went into Preacher's pocket and took the money. Preacher was feeling the heat, so he decided he was gonna need a few heathen friends.

Every Sunday Preacher went to church with his father. One day he told us his father would buy us all kinds of junk if we would come to church that Sunday. The church bus pulled up, and twelve of us got on. It was loaded with candy.

We were all sitting in our seats waiting for the service to begin. This young man with a process (hair style) walked out on stage; he also had on a cape, so I knew we are in for a show. The young man with the process threw his hands in the air twice, and the band hit two notes. He spun around and threw his hands into the air once. The band hit one note, and then the band played and he went into this holy dance and the cape came off.

Then the preacher came out. He was processed up, too. They go at it for about a minute, and then the preacher wiped his forehead with a white hanky and threw it into the second row of pews to this beautiful young lady, and she holds onto it. I also noticed that he made sure that he threw it out of the reach of the big women sitting in the front row. Then he put the cape on James Brown Jr., and he sat down. They went on with the rest of the service. At the end of the service, the young lady that caught the hanky returned it to the preacher, and they talked for a long time. I bet nothing he had to say had anything to do with the

Bible. I began to understand why the mama had to leave him alone.

Sometimes we did stuff and didn't tell the others what we are gonna do it. Bump and go. We were on Imperial and Main. We approached the ice cream truck. Roy bumped up against it with his bike. Roy screamed and fell to the ground. The man driving the ice cream truck came out and attended to Roy. I went inside to get the money box. The driver's kid was in here. He told me I didn't belong in there. I pushed him down and grabbed the money box.

He screamed for his dad. I ran out with the money and jumped on my bike. The others' eyes got big.

The driver said, "What the fuck is happening?"

Then Roy jumped up and got on his bike and the chase was on. I think he was really mad because I took the stash of drugs he was selling off of his truck. He chased us all the way to Lanzit, and then he started shooting at us. We had Preacher with us. I could hear him crying. Anyway we lost him by the canal. When we got back to the projects, Preacher was shaking like a leaf. That was the last time Preacher went anywhere with us.

Junkman Tony

I guess the best way to describe Tony is that he was just an old dirty bastard. He was in the hauling business and well known amongst the other men that worked the construction trade in the Los Angeles area. But what they didn't know about him was that he patrolled the streets of Los Angeles looking for young girls and women under the influence. He would throw them in the back of his truck, and he and his brother would run trains on them.

We were coming back from this dance from Markham one Friday. Roy had to use the restroom so he went in the alley. He spotted junkman Tony's truck and flagged us into the alley.

As we walked up to Tony's truck, he had this young girl way under the influence bent over the bed of his truck. He had her stripped down and about to stick it in when I clocked his ass. We took his big ass down and stomped it. We got her dressed and I took his truck and dropped her off. I then rammed his truck into a pole three times not too far from home.

The wrecked truck and the knots we put on his head were not enough to detour him from raping young girls. A few years later, he was convicted of rape and sentenced to prison.

JACKIE B.

There were some beautiful girls at Markham Junior High when I was going there. The first time I saw Jackie was in the eighth grade. I was walking with Curtis Andrews to class and I looked to the left. She was standing with two other girls.

I said, "Damn, who is that?"

Curtis said, "Man, that's just Jackie." Then we walked a little further and Curtis pointed at Denise Coleman. Debra Mccray, Betty Torrance, Eva Green, Debra Tillman and Cynthia Dent he said those are foxes get it together man. You won't something with some meat on it

I was mesmerized, star struck. I thought she was the most beautiful thing God had ever created. Then she would walk by me every day and just rub it in.

Then in the ninth grade I was placed in the same homeroom with Jackie. She must have put some kind of whammy on me.She had me in a real dangerous spot, It just wouldn't go away. I would stare at her from across the room. All in my thoughts, in my damn dreams, my heart rate would go up. She was the only one to ever get to me like that.

One time she spoke to me, and I broke out in a sweat, lost my voice, and tripped over my feet. My friends knew that I liked her and wanted to help me out. They wrote this letter to Jackie. They couldn't find her so they gave it to her friend Kathleen.

They couldn't figure out what to say to so they took the lyrics from a Smokey Robinson song and used it in the letter. The good thing was they forgot to sign my name at the bottom of the letter saving me from a possible embarrassing moment. They said they had fixed me up and showed me what they had written. The letter said:

> All you have to do is open up
> Your eyes long enough to see that
> You got the love you thought you had in him
> right here in me.you know the song.
> Baby, baby, don't cry.
> Baby, baby, here's why
> Love is here standing by.

Had me sounding like a real desperado

I said, "Unbelievable! Please don't help me again and if they come back at you for information, you don't know nothing."

She was so pretty; she intimidated the hell out of me.

I never gave her any indication that I felt like that.

Right next to where my name should have been they wrote I need you more than Popeye needs his spinach.

The most severe case of love I saw.

This dude named Darnell was crazy about a girl name Pam in the projects. Whenever Pam would break up with Darnell, this fool would lie down in the middle of Imperial Highway and hope that a car would run over him. Cars would swerve trying not to hit him. The only way to get him up was for somebody to go and get Pam. She would tell him it was back on.

On My Way to School

I was on my way to Markham one morning by myself, and I passed by this car and looked in it. The man and the woman were both in the back seat, and the man has his head up under the woman's dress bobbin' like he was bobbin' for apples. I doubled back to make sure what I saw. I was twelve or thirteen. I ain't never seen no shit like that before.

As I was walking to school, I still had this picture in my mind. I didn't want to ask anybody, because they might not believe it. I was trying to figure out what the dude had been doing down there. I asked Roy, and he said he was down there yodeling in the canyon. I said yodeling? Then Roy said that motha-fucka was down there mowing that lawn. I said, "Man, you gonna tell me or not?" When he quit playing and told me, I couldn't believe it.

Markham

I was walking through the lunch area at Markham and accidentally stepped on this dude's shoes. I said "Excuse me" and kept stepping. Apparently that wasn't good enough. He and his friends ran me down. He handed me a rag and told me to get down there and clean his shoes. "I'd rather take an ass-whoopin.' That's not gonna happen." I said.

He was barkin' because he had homeboys standing behind him. He grabbed me. Out of the corner of my eye, I saw my homeboys Charles put me in a position where I had to do something. I turned and threw a left to the nose and a right to the head, and I sat on his chest. I was about to go to work on him, but then I felt someone lift me up by the back of my shirt. It was Mr. Simpson. He snatched us both up. They made us shake hands, take two swats, and then sent us back to class.

I knew it wasn't over. I was on my way home from school the way I usually went, down the tracks. I got halfway down the tracks, and the kid I had the fight came from behind the bushes with two other kids. I guess he wanted a rematch. Then four other kids came from behind the other bushes. It was six kids behind me. Then I realized that I had just walked into a trap.

For some reason I wasn't scared; I probably could have outrun them but I didn't for some strange reason. I put my notebook down and got into a fighting stance. Charles said, "Let's get that bastard.

As they stepped up to me, I was throwing lefts and rights and connecting. I dropped one of them, and they all stayed back. Then they all rushed me and prevented me from using my hands and feet. Then I felt something hit me real hard in the back of my head. I could feel the blood running down the back of my neck. The impact from the blow knocked me to the ground, and they pounced on me. They took turns sitting on my chest and hitting me. I told them they hit like girls, and they tried to kill me. They kicked me, stomped me all in my nuts. Then they ran.

I don't know how long I laid there before I got up. It took me a while to get home. Both of my eyes were the size of golf balls. It took thirty stitches to close my head. They had cracked my ribs and broken my arm. This happened two weeks before we finished the eighth grade. So that is how I finished that school year, at home stitched up.

By July I was just about healed and out running and playing ball. I was waiting on Angel and Roy to get out this summer.

ASS-KICKIN'

Once you get that first real ass-whoopin' and find out that you are not gonna break or die, this fighting thing becomes a whole new ballgame. It happened so fast, I didn't remember faces, and it was hard to see when there were about four or five fists in my eyes.

By the middle of the summer I was just about healed.

Mr. Johnson was too old teach any more. The next best thing was boxing all summer with Vertis. I took a beating in the beginning, but each day I improved. That was what I did all summer: box and play baseball for the W.L.C.A.C.

Charles was the only one I recognized in the group so he bore the burden for the others. I waited all summer for him to come back from down South. Three days before school was to start he came home. I caught him going to the store for his mother. He saw me and ran, but he ran right into Angel and Roy. They had him on the ground fucking him up. I was looking for some lumber. All I could find was a 40-ounce bottle, and I broke it over his head. His eyes rolled back in his head and blood shot out of his head. I thought I had killed him so I ran. I saw him later with his mother in Huntington Park. He had about 50 stitches in his head.We did make him tell us of the others that jumped me.It took a few years but I did to them what they did to me.

A month later, Angel and Roy were sent to Youth Authority long term. I went back to school. I remained that same quiet kid that liked to play sports.

I graduated from Markham. I had had a ball there. I want to thank my teachers, counselors, and friends for everything.

MY FIRST GUN

I was pulling the weeds from the front yard as my mother instructed me to do. Noise from this Monza made me turn around. As I was watching the Monza, it was being closely followed by a police car. Someone in the front passenger seat threw something in a brown paper bag out of the window.

After the police car passed by, I got the brown bag and inside was a.38 revolver and three five-dollar bags of weed. I kept the gun and gave the weed to the others.

A GOOD KID FOR A LONG TIME

For a long time I was a pretty good kid. I did some mischievous stuff and drove some stolen cars. I was the kind of kid that got along with just about everybody. I loved to play ball; that is where I could be found most of the time with Eddie Tunstal, Larry Downs, Sammy Mumphrey, Frank or hanging out with Robby Jones. I didn't get into many fights. Most of the fights I did get into were Angel-inspired.

Angel and Roy were in jail, AL went to Gompers, and the others didn't go to school. Many of the families we grew up with moved away.

I began hanging out on the other side of the projects with Terry Moses, Michael F., Ethan, and Joe Barker. They introduced me to the world of fucking up.

Some people have real negative image of girls from the projects. Most people thought that they were all loud, rude, very little home training, rough, attitude, cuss, alcoholics and addicts,sexually loose. There were a lot of good girls in the bricks smart, talented with dignity and pride and Godly.

CHAPTER 4
BANGIN'

THE CIVIL RIGHTS MOVEMENT

The Civil Rights Movement was in full flow in the 1960s. Many people were doing what they could, and those who couldn't actively participate supported it by other means. The death of Dr. Martin Luther King brought great sadness and uncertainty to black people all across this country. There was anger resulting in riots, destruction, walkouts, and protests. I'm not gonna lie; I didn't understand it all. I knew that there were issues, problems socially, economically, and education that centered on racism.

Something happened between the death of Dr. King and the destruction of the Black Panther Party. Everything changed. We changed. We lost something we haven't been able to get back. We became about the dollar. The cutting of certain social programs and the cutting of certain training and job programs closed a lot of important doors. The lack of positive male images sent a lot of young men to the streets to the wrong kind of man. If young men were not in something positive, it opened up the door for the negative to come in.

This is the period in which the super gangs rose, and young men took to the streets with misdirected anger and in search of something. We turned on each other in that anger and frustration and confusion.

NEXT PHASE

By the time I entered high school, a lot of the friends I had grown up with had moved away. Angel and Roy were in Youth Authority, and Diamond was in camp. I met Tyrone C. years ago when they first moved into the projects. He and the others went to Gompers, and I went to Markham. Now we were all at the same high school.

We formed an alliance, a brotherhood. Tyrone C. and I started the Lot Boys, but I changed the agenda and the course. I thought we should be all that we could be. We formed a bond so thick, we were like brothers. We played football, baseball, and basketball together against other streets and other neighborhoods. We went to parties, school dances, and movies. We took advantage of all that life had to offer. Life was great until that gang shit broke out.

In high school I was a quiet kid when I went to school you really wouldn't have known I was there. I tried to mind my own business and stay out of the bullshit. Most of the time I did what was asked of me in the class room. The high school years were the beginning of the jail years, the get high years.

We did mischievous stuff, like throwing rocks and water balloons at police cars; we smoked weed; drank alcohol; turned the music up; listened to Skillet and Leroy, Rudy Ray Moore. We fought together and against those looking for trouble and to protect the Lot. We even dabbled in a little music.

We had mothers like Mrs. Arlene and Mrs. Carter that opened up their homes to us to keep us off the streets. We couldn't step too far over the line, because we had mothers like Mrs. Sheppard and Mrs. Ivy that would check us.

I was that other kind of kid that came from the projects. I would be on the other side of the projects robbing. In the streets I learned how to fight, steal cars, pull robberies.

My brothers forever, the Lot boys: Tyrone C., JC, KC, Wade, Kenny, Cliff, Squire, Vertis, Jeffery P., Jeffery K., Lee, Joe, George, Curtis, Andre, Tark, Fuzz, Brady, Ronald, Rickey S., Eddie J. and coming up behind us a young: Ralph, DC, DM, DS, and Zack. The high school years were a blur that was the beginning of the banging years, drug and alcohol use, and jail years. Then we had cool and talented brothas like Vic and, Erskine and Steve and his bother Jimmy that hung out with us sometimes. This last line is for the homegirls: chubby, tanchy, Adrian, Shirley, Beverly janet, carrie, Avis, Janet T., Angela, Vickey, Terry, Vonetta, Gloria, Joyce H., Marva.Debra B.,Denise B. Marilyn, Gwen, Annie, Jennie.Gail Brown, Charolette Sheppard, Janet Johnson and Ms. Ivy went home to be with the Lord.

THE BOUNTY HUNTERS GANG

The Bounty Hunters was a gang founded by a committee of brothers, not a few individuals. We were formed or came into existence in self defence of the Crips. Our side of the projects started fighting the Crips before the formation of the Bounty Hunters. We the Lot boys started kicking the Crips ass first; there were only fifteen to twenty of us. We went to school with the Crips, and the Crips began showing up at the place where we were dances, parties and the movies, at the park, and at W.L.C.A.C. It led to a violent confrontation. We hit them hard, sent home all lumped up.

The Crips had had no idea who we were and what they were up against. All they knew was that we were from Nickerson Gardens. In 1971 the Bounty Hunters came out, and we began hitting the Crips at the W.L.C.A.C. People began to talk about the Bounty Hunters. The people that worked at the W.L.C.A.C. began to tell other people about the Bounty Hunters.

The summer of 1972 we fought the Crips just about every day. We beat their ass down, and they'd come back for more, and we'd beat their ass down again. If they didn't show up for us to whoop on, then we would into Crip territory on a search-and-destroy missions. They were easy to identify and I could get right up on them and go to work. When Joe Barker and I got together that was it, Joe meant fuckin business like I did. I could count on Joe and Ethan to show up and be there.

There were a few times when the Crips sent some of us home all lumped up. Everybody lived You went home and soaked your knuckles and got ready for the next time.

It was all about fighting at the time, and it never got more serious than that. They started shooting at us first, and we started shooting back.

The rest of this page is dedicated to some of the originals:

M. Ford, T. Moses, Jr. Thomas, the Barkers Joe, Tony, Gary, Mad Dog, the Spriggs, the Holloways, Hardrock, Hardgrave, Speedy, R. Bryant, the Ortega's, Ba-bra, Frog, David E., L'il J., Farr, Mr. J. Myles, the Trask Brothers, Ernest, Herman, Mr. Dorrough and Mr. Lynch, J. Westbrook, the Greens, Neil, Author P., the Bonners, Cucamonga, J. Smith, J. Noble, A. Sparks a real young Hanky and Squeak, Bill-Bill,Green Eyes, Zorro, the Halls, 109th Park, Hacienda Village, the Teeny Boppers, and others, including my favorite, the Lot Boys and our favorite girl, Sheila Gangster. I didn't want to leave out the little homey CoCo he wasn't a hunter but a homey to the end.

Joe Barker was my favorite Bounty Hunter. May he rest in peace along with Ethan, Roy Lynch, Edward Eley, Rhea, Harold Glen, Calvin Graves, Speedy, and Green Eyes.

We were Nickerson Gardens. We were the neighborhood in which the brothers that formed the Piru, the Athens Park Boys, and the influential members of other gangs came from. Many Crips got their start in the bricks. There were so many Pirus from Nickerson Gardens; you would have thought they were the same gang. They all got their start in the trenches in the bricks.

W.L.C.A.C.

The Watts Labor Community Action Corps: Later on in life when I understood all that Mr. Ted Watkins had accomplished and the circumstances in which he accomplished it all, I was impressed. He became one of the men I wanted to pattern my life after.

If you were a teenager in the 1970s, this was the spot to be. The W.L.C.A.C. brought together teenagers from all over Los Angeles and Compton. To me it was one big party. The one downfall was that it was in Bounty Hunter territory. If you were a Crip, that was your ass. The work wasn't hard. If your not soft, so I knew what hard work was. It was summer, so it was hot. I think the thing I liked the most about the W.L.C.A.C was the marching; you could work and go to Disneyland, Magic Mountain, the beach, and Griffin Park, and it would count as a workday. All the girls, in all shapes and sizes, were all the shades of black.

I joined the W.L.C.A.C. three times and every time I joined I was placed in Mr. Hunter's crew. He was on me every day, every year about something. He would work the shit out of us at Sagus and marched the shit out of us in the sun. He never asked us to do nothing he wouldn't do; he was right there working and marching alongside us. He kept us in check, and he didn't take no shit.

We spent many nights outside our barracks doing pushups by the fifties and jumping jacks by the hundreds for attitude adjustment.

I have nothing but big respect for Mr. Hunter. I understood later on in life that he was trying to mold us into men, respectable, socially aware young men that should be actively involved in the struggle of our people. I didn't stick around long enough to learn more. He kicked me out of his crew three times.I was a banger. I never worried about what may come. I had Wade, Vertis, Jeffrey K., Jeffrey P., Tark, JC, Lee Lewis, D. Johnson, J. Myles, and Reggie, Roni, Rickey, Curtis,Wayne D and the teeny boppers.

Fine ass Jackie was also working there and she is absolutely gorgeous she still walks by me and rubs it in. I peek over there at her once in awhile she still hangs with Kathleen and Christy. I still get a little twisted when I look over there at her I think she put the whammy on me.

BANGIN' I

After the incident at the Hollywood Palladium, the reputation of the Crips skyrocketed. They spread throughout Los Angeles County like a wildfire. It was like a new dance, a new fad, and for bad boys it was the thing to do. Neighborhood after neighborhood began to flip over and become Crips. We were asked to be Crips, and when that offer was turned down, it was war. They stepped up the attacks and we stepped up ours.

We started off fighting the East Side Crips in 1971 from incidents at the W.L.C.AC., the Carver Park Crips. The Compton and West Side Crips were added to the list from incidents at the W.L.C.A.C. and jailed in 1972. When the Jordan Downs and Imperial Courts turned Crip by 1973, we were completely surrounded by the Crips gang.

Our closest allies—the Piru, A.P.B's, Bishops, Gladiators, Vaness Boys, Brims, and Swans—were in the same situation.

DRIVE-BY

One night we were coming back from this Piru party and Diamond's car broke down. We went around the corner to make a phone call and walked into an army of Crips. They were drinking and smoking. They were gonna get us anyway. I just started getting off, throwing lefts and rights. I was hitting them and some of them were falling. I was getting hit, too. There were too many of them. Then more Crips started coming out of this apartment building, coming at us. Now we are backing up, getting hit from all directions. They got two of us on the ground stomping us. I'm still slugging it out.

Thank God Compton Police showed up. I was getting tired; it was twenty on five. The police searched us and made us go separate ways. We came back heavily armed the next day to pick up Diamond's car.

This gang stuff has taken a lot of innocent lives. It has also destroyed a lot of relationships, friendships, communities on lockdown, and borders. Some of us from Nickerson Gardens swam, played baseball for Carver Park, and knew the brothers from Mona Park we played against. We went to Markham with the brothers and the sisters from the Jordan Downs and Imperial Courts. It's tragic; now we were fighting like cats and dogs.

We had been hitting the Crips real hard all summer.

I wasn't there but while some of us were getting high and drinking, the Crips rode down on us and fired about fifteen rounds, but they missed. That same night the Crips hit us. I wanted to ride down on them but the police were everywhere.

My boy Diamond pulled up in a stolen car, and we hopped in. We parked down the street from this Crip party. We sat in the car and got buzzed. The Crips had just finished stomping these two dudes outside the party. I took two more pulls off of the joint and told Diamond, "Let's ride."

Diamond pulled alongside them, and I jumped out of the car. I shot the one closest to me and blasted another one, and they ran. I jumped back in the car. Al was with us. He froze and threw up in the backseat. I think we were done with Al at this point, and he was done with us. He choked. The Crips rode down on us again, and they missed again.

Two weeks later I knew where I could find Crips. They hung out by this store. We went through our ritual, the smoking of the peace pipe, killing a forty. We parked across the street and watched them.

We had them boxed in. Diamond was parked across the street.

I went into store. They stood up and jawed at me. There were about twelve of them. I ignored them. I went in, removed the gun from my coat, and came out of the exit blastin'. The first one to get it was the fat motha-fucka doin' all the talking. Then I dropped these other two, and the rest took off running. They ran right into Roy and Diamond they were lucky the pump jammed. I reloaded and pursued the ones that got away. Them niggas was fast. The cops were all over our neighborhood that night and the next night. They wanted to shoot. We shoot.

We lived on Zamora and at night when we were out there hanging out we had to be on full alert to prevent ourselves from being a victum of a drive by.If you drove into our lot to slow or drove by more than once. There were probably several guns pointed at you if you flinched that was your ass.

PARTY I

Diamond was invited to a party by a girl he met at a burger stand, and he asked us to roll with him. We went in three cars. I think there were eleven of us. I told them we went inside to behave with none of that project shit. The party was jumpin' women everywhere.

We go through our rituals and I make a bathroom run. Mumbles was coming out as I was going in, and he was laughing. I asked him what he did. We went back into the bathroom, and Mumbles pulled back the shower curtains, and there were three shitty towels in the bathtub.

I said, "Gene you took these people's good damn towels and wiped your ass with them?"

He said, "I sure fuckin did, didn't you always?"

I said, "My mind doesn't work like that." I made him throw the towels out of the window.

Shit man and myself went back down stairs.

Then the others started cutting up. They were in this girl's kitchen frying steaks, and they had gone through these folks' bar and drunk up their good alcohol.

On making phone calls to Texas and down South, girls started leaving, because some of the brothas were rude. When the couch went up in smoke, they asked us leave.

Some protesters were standing across the street. They wanted to talk to us about the way we behaved in the party; you know, to straighten us out. There were about thirty of them and eleven of us. The little short nigga who was doing all the barkin' called us over to where they were standing, so we walked over there. From where I was standing, I saw that he had his .25 automatic drawn, and all of us were strapped.

Before we got there, half of them ran. When we got up close, the others saw us heavily armed and seven more took off. We got up close and he asked us, "Where you niggas from?"

Roy said, "Nickerson Gardens," and the last two took off. So it was just the short nigga and his mouth. He was singing a different song then.

I told him, "You done fucked now. You're gonna have to hump the pole. I said, 'See that telephone pole over there? Get your ass over there and start humpin put your arms around that motha—fucka and kiss.'"

He resisted and I went upside his head with the .38, and he went over there and got busy.

PARTY 2

Our homeboy Jo-Jo invited us out to this party in Pacoima. It was nice; everyone behaved themselves. It was about two in the morning when we were on our way back home. I was in the back tore up and damn near asleep. Roy and Diamond were up front. Gene was in the back with me.

This black Continental pulled alongside us, looked in our car, and hit us with some hand signs Crip signs. I was trying to get up under the seat and get my gun, but it was too late. They started busting on us and drove off. Diamond damn near ran into two other cars.

We got off of the freeway and did damage check. Diamond got cut up from the glass, and he didn't have any windows on the left side. We went into the trunk, broke out with the equipment, and got back on the freeway to hunt them down. It took us fifteen minutes to find them. They were cruising, blasting their music. I told Diamond to pull alongside them, and when he pulled even I took the .38 and the automatic and revolver and emptied both in that car. Bounty Hunters.

EVEN THOUGH

When I got out this time, I wasn't scared anymore. I wasn't bashful anymore. I surprised the hell out of myself. I knew it was in me somewhere. I think the thing that made me angry was the girls that thought they were too good for you or wouldn't have anything to do with you. Now two kids and a hundred pounds later, they are all over you. I don't mess with the home boys' girls even when they break up with them. That shit ain't right. And you don't mess with your homeboy's girl while he is in jail, either.

Bangin' 3

When the banging started hitting the headlines every week and the death toll started skyrocketing, society saw it as a problem, a small problem that if, given time like all other fads, would pass. The young men that started the different gangs had no idea that what they started would reach the level or magnitude that it reached.

The population of Juvenile Hall began to quadruple, and Youth Authority doubled up. Young men began to enter the prison system by the droves.

In hopes of saving their sons, some mothers packed them up and shipped them off to Job Corps or down South or back East. A change of scenery didn't change what had been planted deep within them. Wherever they went, they recruited and spread that influence.

The influence of the L.A. gangs hit the South, Northwest, and Midwest with the same enthusiasm as it had hit L.A. They embraced it, and it took root and spread. The brothers from back East began to move out here and sign up. When they went back East, they spread it.

With gang-banging came a lifestyle, a line of clothing, shoes, hats, coats, and hangout spots, along with groupies and supporters. The gangs had their own language and sign language. This was where it all began, with the bangers of the early 70s. It set them all apart from other groups.

In the juvi system the Crips had us outnumbered 200 to 4 another time about 300 to 8. As far as the blood gangs there were more Bounty Hunters in juvi than any other blood gang.The other blood gangs watched us stand in the juvi,camp, youth authority system and the other blood gangs began to stand with us. I have so much respect for Vop, LB, Diallo from the Piru, J. Mcgowan from the Brims, R. Walker from the A.P.B'S, Peanut and Red from the Gladiators and Flake from the Bishops they stood in the midst of the storm.A lot of the eastside Crips showed me a lot of respect because of my cousin T.,Tyrone.This line is for five of the bravest youngsters I have ever met Ba—Bra and Butter Red, R Bryant, T. Barker and Frog they made me proud.

Jealousy and revenge, stupidity are the monsters that fuel this thing called bangin they blot out everything.They find a place in your heart and mind and hold on.This last line is for my homeboy and classmate George Henderson my friend's life was taken from him he was a victim of gang violence.He wasn't a banger he was a kid that like to have fun and he was alot of fun to be around.Rest in peace.

CHAPTER 5
DOG

NEW BEGINNING

I paroled to Los Angeles, and I was living with Royce and Duck in a two bedroom apartment on the west side. They both were rarely there; when they were, it was a tragedy. To get to the kitchen, I had to step over butt-naked drunk and drugged-up women, and beer and whiskey bottles. Every day there was a sink full of dirty dishes, and clothes all over the place.

My parole officer was cool. All he asked was that I test clean and stay out of trouble. BB was looking for me. He was ready to put his plan into action. We met at this popular soul food restaurant to discuss the details. He told me he had been giving me bits and pieces of the game since I was a kid, sending me on missions. He said my time was now.

To put some money in our pockets, we hit a few dope houses and then Sundown set up a few road trips for us. This was when I meet big Onion. He was called Onion because of the shape of his head.

Our first stop was to Oakland; our last to Seattle. After all of that riding, you got stiff and tired. I enjoyed seeing all of these places. Under normal circumstances, I would not have gotten a chance to see them.

In Seattle, we handled business, got rooms for the night to rest and prepare for the long ride home in the morning. Big Onion had too much to drink and smoke last night and was paying for it the next morning. Roy and I went across the street to get coffee and donuts and on our way back, I saw two masked men at our car, probably jacking Onion. We had to sit and watch it play out, so it wouldn't turn into a shoot-out and draw heat.

The driver was parked down the street the plan was to not let them make it to their car. We crossed the street, already strapped. After the robbers got the money, they took off the ski masks and walked toward us. As we approached each other, we spoke and I swung around and went upside the big one's head with my gun. I hit his ass again, and I beat on him some more while he was on the ground. The other one pissed on himself and started crying, "Don't kill me."

I got the money back. They were very lucky we were in kind of a public place. When I saw what he did to Onion,

I started to go back and get them. We just went home instead.

JUMP

We jumped into BB's ride and rode over to the other side of town to meet the man that makes it all go. We pulled up to this where house where these old dudes were on the side playing bid wiss.

The one they called uncle said to bring us in. Uncle Bobby said, "I have heard a lot about you both since you were kids." About three men brought in two junkie-looking bastards.

I heard Uncle Bobby say, "This can't wait." He walked up to the fat one and removed the gun from the middle of his back and went upside the fat one's head with it. He turned on the pigmy-looking one and beat him down to the ground. Uncle Bobby used drug addicts as his eyes and ears on the streets. When they failed him he punished them severely.

Then Uncle Bobby lit up a cigar and sat down in his easy chair. He told the fat one to take the rake in the corner and beat the pigmy with it. The fat one beat the pigmy like he had stolen something.

Uncle Bobby told him to stop and give him the rake. He then gave the pigmy a machete and told him to cut the fat bastard up for beating him. Fat boy took off, and Pigmy was right behind him. Uncle Bobby was watching this like he watched television. He was really enjoying it.

Pigmy never caught the fat one, because he got tired. Then Uncle Bobby pulled out a small package of heroin, and their eyes lit up. They both begged him for a fix. Pigmy and the fat boy were crying, saying they would do anything for a fix. Everyone was laughing, except me. I didn't see the humor in it.

Uncle Bobby told the fat one to get off his fat ass and suck Pigmy off, and he did. I went into the other room. I heard Uncle Bobby tell Pigmy, "All right, you little runt bastard, it's time for you to get your tonsils tickled. Get your ass down there and suck like a vacuum cleaner." Pigmy got down and got busy. They all laughed and applauded. It wasn't the act it was to see out of desperation if they would do it to break the spirit of a man.

Uncle Bobby opened up the package of heroin and poured it all over the ground and laughed. The two junkies scrambled for it, and everyone laughed at them.

They all came into the room where I was and looked at me. I had my hand on my gun, because I didn't know whose turn it was to suck the next dick. They didn't think I had the stomach for the business. Ain't nothing scary about me; I just didn't want to see two men suck each other off.

"You quiet motha-fuckas the worst kind," Uncle Bobby said. "It is with your secret sins. You have shed a lot of blood, too, in your own way. I know about you. The power I have one day, you will have, too, and the longer you have it, the colder you become. I like you, kid. You remind me of myself."

Then I heard about three or four gunshots go off. Uncle Bobby took another swig of whiskey and chased the dick suckers around the warehouse shooting at them. I told BB that that motha-fucka was retarded. BB said, "When you get to know him, you will understand him. The man is brilliant when it comes to this shit. Uncle Bobby's father did the same thing to us when we were your age."

Sundown came over to Roy and me and shook our hands. He was the one who had set up all of our road trips. That was his role.

Uncle Bobby was special. He used to sit in his chair, fire up a cigar, and have women freak off in front of him. Line strangers off of the streets up against the wall and throw darts, rocks, baseballs, and shoot arrows at them. The thing that gave him his biggest chuckle was having two drunken winos fight each other. He did the same thing with animals, too.

Uncle Bobby had a son named Larry. They called him Low Down. Low and his boys used to cruise the bus stops, train stations, and back alleys for homeless and runaway girls. They would get them strung out on drugs and put them to work. Sometimes Low and his boys would run trains on them. Everything he did was for show or so that he could be seen. Like his father, he pitted people against each other in order to be entertained.

He couldn't stand me, just like I couldn't stand his ass. I was too big for him to whip, so he had to tolerate me. It was like dealing with the boss's son at work who holds an important position that he doesn't deserve. He was there only because his daddy owned the company.

When Uncle Bobby went to jail, Low Down thought he was next in line to run the show. They called him Low Down for a reason; his ass was dirty. He stole from his own father, made deals on the side with his father's competitors, and burned other dealers. When his life was on the line, his daddy would bail him out. Low and his boys tried to overthrow BB, who said, "Punish him, but don't put him down." We sent him packing with a few lumps.

On the west side, I would see things that stirred up feelings that I tried to suppress. I would see fathers and sons interacting with each other, going to games, fathers cheering their sons from the bleachers, fathers coaching their sons. I also saw wisdom and opportunities up close being passed down.

West Side

On the west side, I was exposed to a lot more and I saw how I wanted to live. When my first dream disappeared, I had to come up with another one. I didn't feel I could accomplish that dream through education or hard work. Money and power have a way of corrupting you.

BB was driving me through the different areas where we did business in his Lincoln, pointing out the troublemakers, rats, and telling about certain people and their backgrounds.

In my opinion, they had been too polite been too friendly. That was why they kept coming up short, losing territory, getting played by ho's. It was a business, and you had to run it like a business. That was all about to change.

There were a few that got stubborn on us. What I did was take out my gun and knock out their front teeth or shoot them in a leg. This one O.G. said he wasn't moving. We swooped on him at about eleven o'clock as he was going home. We picked him up and tortured him in the car. Then I kicked his ass out of the car while it was still moving.

The next line of business was to deal with all the little independents out there cutting into our business. Many chose to just roll it up rather than meet the same fate the others met; those who stood their ground were squashed like bugs. The word got around real fast.

The hostile takeover took about two weeks. They got mad at me because I wouldn't bring any women into the picture. Women can be a distraction they require attention and this is business.

My goal was to make all of the money I could from the business and get out. I didn't want to be Number One or move to the next level. I just wanted to pull myself up out of this hole, because I knew there's more. I was just a ranked soldier in BB's army of convicts. I'd seen men invest many years in the business and walk away with nothing or put in more time in jail than they have on the streets. The life expectancy rate was short, and the job benefits were overrated.

Angel was getting out after serving six years. We were waiting at the gate for him, when he came out with this big grin on his face. I had my own place now, and I fixed the other room up for Angel to live in, and I bought him a car. I knew it was the middle of the week, but we threw this big party for him and invited women from all over. The party was nice; we were playing some of that KG.F.J. music, talking about the past. Once Angel made his selection, the party was short. He headed toward his room with a honey and a bottle of wine. The main thing was that he was home.

THE CREW

I had been gone a while, so everyone had gone in different directions trying to make it in this world. If I was gonna roll, I wanted my boys' pockets to be fat, too, regardless what BB said. I had to have somebody around me I knew and trusted. I chose lock unit convicts because they didn't give a fuck about nothin.

Once everything was in place, it was time to bring my boys into the picture. Ghost was on the phone in an office making an insurance pitch to some lady. He saw me and put the "Out to Lunch" sign up and never went back.

Duck was in a restaurant in back busting suds when I walked in the back and said, "Let's go."

Mumbles was delivering furniture for a company when I found him. He told me his wife would kill him if she caught him talking to me. I said, "Man or mouse, motha-fucka." He got in the car.

Diamond was working as a mechanic at a fat dude's auto place. Fat boy was always on DJ about something; a lot of it was jealousy. He saw me and walked right off the job.

Tank was home collecting G.R. and turning himself into an alcoholic.

Skip was sweeping the floor of a grocery market complaining about how fucked up his life was, taking all kinds of abuse from the public and from store management. I said, "You ready to roll? Get out of that apron."

Roy was at a big gambling shack with Big Hershey when I caught him.

I was not big on speeches. I kept it brief and to the point. I ran the program down, the dangers and the rewards. Then I laid the rules out and why we needed them.

They were not happy about the rules, but you couldn't have people around you just doing whatever they wanted and attracting heat, creating confusion from within. The key was to follow instructions and keep your mouth closed.

Big Hershey

When BB introduced Hershey to me for the first time, he told me without asking me that he would be like my advisor, teacher, and instructor. Any and every thing I would need to know about the game, he would teach me.

Hershey looked me up and down and said, "Image is important. That hat and vest with no suit shit you like to wear and jeans with Stacy's, we are gonna switch it up. I need you sharp, even if it is casual, not street thug." He was right I made myself a target.

I was a little embarrassed, not that I thought I knew it all, but this was the second time he had talked down to me like a kid. Once we got past the bullshit and the ego trip, I found out Big Hershey was all right. He's about thirty years older than I am, but he passed for a forty-year-old. He had been to the joint three times. He was shot in both legs once and left to die in the desert.

What he brought to the table was organizational skills and vision. They had a ten-year plan; I had a two-year plan. He took me on as his personal project. He thought my personality, patience, and manner of speech were perfect for the situation.

It took my all to keep from knocking the shit out of him a few times. Oh, yeah, I forgot he said I had this thing about women all twisted. His exact words were, "You must have taken classes in ho sympathizing or Save a Ho 101. What are we doing? Are we pimpin' or selling drugs?"

Later on, as we progressed, I understood what he was preparing me for. It didn't register at first, but then it passed before me like a parade one day. We had one ho fuck up half our crew and try to work me.

Hershey told BB, "I ain't never met a nigga like that motha-fucka in there. No strip club, no tit bar, no clubs, no drink and drive, no orgies, and. What's wrong with that motha-fucka fishing, reading, riding a fucking bike, quiet?"

BB said, "That's why I chose him. He's a fucking beast when he has to be, and he has control over his emotions. You will never see him out of character."

This shit is just as deep as it is crooked and just as crooked as it is deep. I hated it, it depressed me. I knew what we were doing to our communities. The others they didn't give ah fuck they were impressed with the money and loved the life style and the attention

They were living their dream money, fancy cars, women,a house.

WOMEN

For a long time I was bashful, still scared of girls, and couldn't even hold a decent conversation with one without breaking into a sweat. When I got out of jail, I was seventeen, and something rolled out with me. It was different. I think they sensed it, too.

Years later after getting some more corruption under my belt and sitting under the influence of drug dealers and gangsters, I began to see women in a different light. I began to incorporate their philosophies into the program. Some women liked me until they found out my ass was bad.

When we started doing our thing out here, I had to change the way I dressed, how I fixed my hair, and what I drove, and who I was seen with. Big Hershey said no slouching, that I was to lead by example. I was not a show-off, and I didn't like a lot of attention. I could pass for a prep school college student it worked. Then Big Hershey said not to get fucked up behind these ho's, that I "should keep in mind if you wasn't rolling the way you was, they be as giving or all over me? You really don't want to think about what side of the fence they are going to be standing when you go to jail. Jump to the next one that flows. It's a game. Keep them at a distance. Fuck love and romance and all that other silly shit. Gangsters don't fall in love. Fuck marriage. Fuck a commitment." You can't trust a bitch.

He saw the look in my eyes that it didn't register. He repeated, "It's us versus them. Winner takes all. Just get the pussy. I carried out the program to the full extent. I probably ran off some good women in doing so. I didn't let them in. I kept them at a distance."

Hershey was convinced that there wasn't a woman on this planet you could trust or could truly love him for who he is.

I understood what he said to a certain extent. When you're out there doing wrong where love is, there is a tendency to stay on the streets with your girl. Some men that are close to their girls have a tendency to share the corrupt and violent things we do with them, because of that closeness. That is a no-no. The danger is if you break it off, she is gonna be on the stand trying to put us all away to get back at you. That I understood.

FRIENDS

Some kids can be raised in the projects and not be distracted or fall to all of the negative things and influences going on around them.

Some of the brothas and sistas I grew up with on Zamora went on and did well I was so proud of them.

After I got out of jail, I tried to catch up with some of my friends that I grew up with. Some of them really struggled their first couple of years out of high school, trying to find their place in this world. Some of them moved away; some of the brothas went into the service; and some of the girls were called into motherhood. Some went to junior college or trade schools; others got jobs at markets and warehouses.

Fat face he was. The little fat kid on our street that went to school every day was in a lot of school clubs. He was friendly and smart. He didn't bang. He stayed away from drugs and alcohol and went to church every Sunday. There were a lot of good kids like him in the projects.

He looked up to me, but I really admired him. He was a dedicated husband and father. He worked an eight-hour job and was going to college at night. That wasn't easy. When I saw him interacting with his children, it always did something to me.

He knew what I did for a living, but he never let that come between us. He always had something encouraging to say to me.

PEOPLE

There are people who like to get high but don't have the money to do so. They will let you come into their home and set up shop, do whatever you need to do. As long as you get them off, some of the big girls think that dick comes with the use of their facilities.

The sneaky ass females would watch where they would stash the drugs, and then call the police and my boys would have to leave some of the stuff and go. These females would come out and grab the drugs and go back into their apartment. They burned us twice until we figured it out.

The men that answered to me, some of them were twice my age and looked at me with curiosity. The stories they heard about me didn't fit my personality.

Just like any other group, we had a few problems. Some of the brothas I had to get rid of the same day I hired them. Some of them refused to follow instructions; some couldn't control their hormones. I can't stand men that mess with under-aged girls, or using drugs on girls to rape them. There were problems with jealousy with job duties. Some of the men felt they should have been given more responsibility, more power in leadership positions. Some of the men got hooked on drugs. Falling in love will fuck you up, too.

Then you have men feeding information to the police and your rivals, men that would cross you for a few dollars, making arrangements with your enemy. Some things I want talk about how you deal with treachery I won't mention in this book.

AT NIGHT

I had progressed from the business and had all that a reasonable man could want and more than I knew what to do with. I lived in a big lonely house by myself. Some nights I slept for three or four hours, and then I would hop up. I was always on post. The slightest noise made me reach up under my pillow for my gun. I was opposed to having bodyguards anywhere. I had received a lot of threats, and my list of enemies quadrupled. I had all kinds of nightmares, dreams of people after me. I slept with a gun under my pillow and another one under my mattress, a 30-30 Winchester in my closet, and a 30 aught 6 nearby. I knew how to make house calls, too.

Preacher 2

When Preacher moved away, he stayed in contact with us heathens and said we were always in his prayers. The day he was ordained as a pastor, he wanted us all to be there to share that moment with him. As many of us that could make it pulled suits and ties out of our closets and headed out to Riverside, California. I was proud of him; one of us going to another level in anything.

When we got there, the ushers greeted us with open arms, and the girls couldn't take their eyes off us. They gave us the 'ooh, thugs' look. They seated us right up front.

The part of the service to ordain Preacher took about twenty minutes, and then he was given the mike to preach his message. It was about life and death, blessings and curses, probably directed at us. At the end of his message, he called us all up to the altar and shared a few project stories. He prayed the sinners' prayer with us and prayed over us.

Afterwards, we all went into a big room and had lunch and fellowship. We talked for a couple of hours and then went home. At the church picnic that we all came to because of the women, we were all baptized in Lake Perris. Two of the brothers that came with us met their future wives there.

These same two brothers began to pull back from us, stopped putting in street time. They wanted a family and to be married. They didn't want to die young or be locked up. They didn't have to tell me. I knew, and I didn't want to get in the way of that.

Preacher was dispatched to Arkansas to replace a pastor there who had recently passed away.

Sometimes I Wish

Sometimes I wish I could go back before there were gangs and corruption and selling drugs, and do it again. I wanted to graduate with my friends Eddie and Larry and my other classmates play baseball in high school with them. I don't know if the others sleep at night or not, but I don't. When I do sometimes I have nightmares. I constantly have my hand on the trigger when your living close to death that is what you do.

I know that at any given moment, without seeing it coming, someone could walk up to me and take my head off and end it all. Would I be missed? Maybe, maybe not, but that is not how I want to go out. Right now I don't see any other way out, and I want to step away without Roy or Angel or the others. And I'm tired of cleaning up everybody's fuck ups.

I opened this door. I guess I have to be the one to close it. I hear the voice of my grandmother lately saying she didn't raise me like that.

Last Straw

Too much blood was being spilled, and at the rate we were going, we were going to end up with life sentences or on death row. That dam Angel ain't no fuckin joke. I told the crew that we were going to come off the streets and take the show on the road. All we had to do was to make sure everything got where it had to go.

That didn't mean there wasn't any treachery. The brothers from other states were real jealous of the brothers from Cali. Some of them pretended they liked us, but they really couldn't stand us. When we made our out-of-state runs, sometimes there was some shit in the game. They set you up to get robbed, followed you back to the hotel, came back with five or six of their stick-up boys, and set up an isolated spot to meet to attempt to rob you.

The easiest set-up was four or five ho's inviting guys upstairs to party. While everybody was getting high, one of them would slip away, unlock the door, and let an army of thugs in to jack the place. None of that ever happened to us, because it was all about business: drop and go.

We celebrated when we got back home. Angel didn't have a lot of patience away. His ass would exterminate'. We never lost a dime or an ounce. They were fucking with the wrong niggas thinking about robbery. I won't even tell you how we dealt with treachery and the attempts to rob us or shortchange us. It ain't nice.

One day I just walked away never looked back without the others.

CHAPTER 6
THE COUNTY JAIL

THE COUNTY JAIL

The county jail is a very cold and lonely place. If you're at all claustrophobic or bashful, you might have problems trying to make the adjustment. You're in a cell with four to six other men. You always have an audience; there is nothing that you do that they don't see.

The county jail at that time was open for you to interact with the other prisoners; in other words you could go to the other prisoners' cells and play cards and dominoes and socialize. We were not on constant lockdown. We were on our way back from court and were put in this holding tank waiting to catch the chain back to the county.

The holding tank was right across from the queen tank or where they had the homosexuals. I heard someone from the homosexual tank all dressed in drag call my name, "Johnny Blair." I looked at this man in a dress, makeup, and wig, and said to myself, 'I don't know anybody like that.'

This dude said to me, "You probably don't recognize me like this but my name is Donald Davis. We went to Markham together."

I said that I remembered. I wanted to ask him what happened, but before I could ask him he told me, "I've been a bitch all my life. I had to hide it because of the way they treated queens in the Watts area, beating, stabbing, and killing them. Then he asked me, "Is that P over there?" I said, "That sure is, P went over there and put his thing in that man's mouth. I thought it was some pretty foul shit touching another man.

"P said Johnny, I used to have that hang-up, too," "One night when I was in Youth Authority, they were turning this dude out and I was laying there on my bunk listening. P said 'When I heard that grease jar being opened making that noise that it makes when you opened it'. 'I heard that grease poppin' in his ass. My shit got rock hard."

I said, "it doesn't matter I'm still not touching another man."

Then P said, "It ain't nothing a little soap and water can't handle.".Some men don't feel that there is anything wrong with touching another man as long as they are the fucker and not the fuck-ee.

Roy and I were in the same jail tank, and sometimes we would see Angel and Diamond in the chow hall. We met sometimes in church service to discuss our case.

This big angry-looking black man about 6'4" and about 350 pounds came into our tank. Roy followed him into his cell, and they got into a heated discussion. I was thinking I might have to help Roy with this one; this dude was huge.

Roy slapped him, and I jumped up. This big grizzly grabbed his face, started crying and covered up. He said, "I'm sorry, Roy. I'll get your money."

Then I saw Roy grab him by his ear down to his cell. Roy said, "Get your ass ready I've got a few tricks lined up."

Then this giant stripped down and gets ready. Several men one at time came into that cell and paid that fool to sleep with him. I was in shock. This big ass bear was down on the meat trombone. I have to say it he got Roy's money Angel and Roy were some wild niggas; I could see this was gearing up to be one wild ride.

Then you'd get into stuff in there behind the stuff you did on the streets. This young man wanted to fight me. He had his little weapon, a razor melted onto a toothbrush. That wasn't gonna stop me from fucking him up. I anticipated stuff like this. I knew I had a large fan club.

I went in my cell to get something, and he tried to flank me from the back. I turned and I grabbed his arm with razor and bent it all the way back. Then I took my free hand and cracked him real good. He fell back on the way down and hit his head on the toilet and fell out, bleeding.

It cost me ten days in lockup, because somebody told on me.

Then I got into another incident with this convict about thirty-five, and they put this semi-retarded young man in his cell. For about two weeks he'd been trying to fuck my card partner and manipulate him out of his money. One day I was ready to play cards and was waiting on my partner to show up. I went down to his cell to see what was wrong, and Jared was sitting on the floor crying. I asked him what was wrong, and he said Tony sexually abused him.

I got mad and went down that cell where Tony was shooting the shit with his fellow players. Angel said to the others, "Get the fuck out!" They ran out of that cell. To make the story short, Tony had to go to the hospital when we were done.

Then you'd see stuff in the county jail that was unbelievable. This white dude was leaning up against the wall smoking and talking to himself. He then stepped onto the middle of the tier, did a few stretches, and walked all the way to the back of the tier. Then he got down like he was coming out of a starting block and took off into a full sprint. He was running from the back of the tier to the front of the tier at Olympic speed. I thought that if he generated enough speed when he hit the bars, they would fall down. He hit the bars at full speed and they laid his ass out. The MTAs came band picked up what was left of him. It took about an hour to mop up all of the blood.

We were sitting in the holding tank after hearing all of the evidence against us at our pre-trial. Our attorneys came to us with a deal: we had to plead guilty to one of the charges for five to eight years for them to drop the rest. I had to plead guilty to assault with a deadly weapon. If I took it to trial and lost, I could be sentenced to up to twenty-five years. So we talked it over and all agreed to take the deal.

Two weeks later, we were scheduled to be sentenced. Being that the county jail was open at that time, you heard the great storytellers like Noah do their thang. He kept us entertained many nights with his Richard Pryor impersonations and many others. When he was done, the lights went off, and then it was Roy's turn to step up to the mike. He was so talented; he had the men jumping, hollering and dancing in their cells, and then he always finished with a touching ballad. I sat there and looked and listened in amazement; so would the guards.

Duck and Ghost were sentenced to Youth Authority; they were first timers. The rest of us were given prison terms.

I don't blame my mother, and I don't blame my father. I don't use them as an excuse for failing. It was my fault I chose this path. I just prayed that the ride is not too long or too bumpy. I have heard some shit about Tracy, D.V.I.

COUNTY JAIL III

That same night they brought in Buck, and he saw stuff that wasn't there. His cousin said Buck was trying to get from up under all this time by playing crazy to get into a mental institution. He was doin' a damn good job, too. On our way to breakfast Buck dropped his shorts and shit in the middle of the tier and then smeared it on the wall and rolled around in it. They shut the place down and carried his ass out of there in a straightjacket.

Then we got Drew, a college kid who refused to pay his tickets and challenged the system and lost. They gave him seven days. A product of a mixed marriage, he had gone to prep schools all of his life. He spoke like he was educated, so niggas with only a fifth grade education were offended when he spoke. He was my new card partner and was scared to death of the niggas in here. I bet he won't refuse to pay his tickets anymore.

COUNTY JAIL FOUR

In there once in a while you'd run into someone you grew up with or went to school with. Some of them were glad to see you, and some of them, out of embarrassment, tried to duck, overlooking that you gave them the heads up on the place and let them know it was gonna be alright, and if something came up, get back at me.

There was rat-packing where the mice were the majority. At that time in the county jail, they threw everybody together: killers, bangers, crippled, robbers, pick-pockets, and people in for misdemeanors. The weak were preyed upon.

My list of enemies was long from banging, taking the cars of other young men, turning-out parties, just fuckin up, the dirty shit we did during the drug years.

You did so much shit you didn't remember faces or where to begin, but they never forgot your ass. Your name would pop up, and they would say where that motha-fucka at? When they realized that you were not a little fella, most backed off, but some didn't.

Half of the time I didn't know who my enemy was. I walked past this dude, and he socked me in the back of the head. It hurt him more than it hurt me. I spun around and said, "You done fucked up." I tore into his ass. I had him on his back fucking him up. They pulled me off of him. Roy said the guards were coming to take count, so we went back into our cell.

When we came out to finish, he had stripped down to his shorts and was all greased up. The grease was so I couldn't grab him. I picked up where I left off. I stomped his ass to send a message to the others. He was all fucked up. He didn't want to, but he needed a doctor. He didn't stop bleeding so he had to leave the tier to get medical help.

Then the cops came on our tier and conducted a knuckle and blood search. I had blood on my clothes, and my knuckles were all messed up. I was cuffed and taken to lockup. I didn't give a fuck.

THE L.A. COUNTY JAIL—B

Today one of my girls came to see me. I didn't lie to them about certain things, and I told them based on the testimony of one man I was gonna be gone for awhile. I was not gonna hold you up but they insisted in hanging in there.

I went back to the tank. There was a dice game going on in the back cell, the poker players playing poker and pimps and players collectively together. We had jailhouse attorneys in there helping some of the men with their cases.

The church brothers got together in the back or in a cell and have church, studying God's word. I understood that people slip and fall, and they fall and slip.

Most of the men there were between the ages of eighteen and twenty-three which means that what happens after high school was critical. There was a need for stronger mentoring programs and accountability programs. Some of the men shouldn't have been there.

Some of the men there genuinely found Christ and went to serve him with all of their heart in many capacities in the prison system and many of them were hard core bangers. Some of the men mocked God, made all kinds of promises to God from this dungeon; their decision to serve God was based on the outcome of their case.

I thought it would be hypocritical to call upon God when I was living like a devil. There was no television to watch or radio to listen to; we had to entertain ourselves. Vaboom would do his Mr. Richard Pryor impersonations and rock it. Then Roy would step

Up and sing and rock the house he always ended with a ballad

FIGHT

This dude Jerome in our tank had been telling the other brothers in our tank he couldn't stand me, and if I so much as flinched in his direction he was gonna fuck me up. He said that I had shot up his homeboys. Anything was possible. I had already received my time, and I could leave from a regular cell or lock-up and go to Chino it doesn't matter.

I was on my way to a visit, and we passed each other as I came out of my cell. I think he bumped into me on purpose. He looked at me and said something, and he came out of his shirt. I was getting ready move on him, and Angel grabbed me and said to go to my visit.

I told Jerome we would continue this when I got back. I came back from my visit thirty minutes later, and on my way to the back of the tier Jerome sprang out on me from where he was hiding. He let me pass by, and then he jumped on my back like a wild man. He stuck his fingers in my eyes, and I threw his ass on the ground. He sprang back like a cat and leaped on me again. Jerome wrapped his legs around my waist and his arms around my head trying to twist it off.

I start hitting him with body shots, and he let go of my head and tried to grab my hands. He leaped forward and head-butted me, and then he started biting me hard. I picked him up and ran him into the bars. He hit the ground and leaped up once again to attack. He ran into a left and a right and hit the ground and stayed down. I walked over to him and kicked him across his face for biting me. That was like fighting a cat monkey.

They moved him to another tank. Angel came over and congratulated me and introduced me to this giant name Ferocious.

CHAPTER 7
THE JOURNEY

CHINO—THE RECEPTION CENTER

Four days after being sentenced, the L.A. county sheriffs carried us in chains to the reception center in Chino. It was decided there where you would do your time. You were officially processed into the prison system; your picture was taken; and you were given a number by the state (the brand of slavery). The number was what you would be known as. You were fingered-printed and went to classification. They looked over your file; discussed what was in the file with you; and you were assigned a cell.

For some of the men there it was their third or fourth trip to the joint. They acted like being there was nothing; happy to be there; getting some sex, a good meal, and a return home. Me, I was devastated. As you walked the yard you wanted to kick yourself in the ass. I saw myself doing a lot of things in my life and in my dreams prison wasn't one of them. I don't blame anyone but myself.

One week later we were awakened by banging of a club on our bars around three o'clock in the morning. I was told to roll it up; I was headed up north. My cell door was racked or opened, and I stepped out with all of my belongings. We were fed and put in a holding cell. Thirty minutes later we were stripped, searched, and given white pants and top to put on and placed back in the holding cell.

Twenty minutes later, six guards that look like linebackers called us out of the cell two at a time to chain us up. A chain goes around your waist; cuffs are attached to the chain the cuffs go around your wrist, so your hands are cuffed to your waist. Then a chain with cuffs is attached to your ankles so you can't run.

Then we sat down and waited some more. The guards showed up again for roll call. As our names were called, we were loaded onto this bus called the Grey Goose.

As one of the men was stepping on the bus, he tripped because of the chains. The guards jumped him. They said he was trying to escape. One of the Mexican dudes that was already on the bus yelled something; he called them dogs. One of the redneck guards stepped onto the bus and said, "Who said that?" Nobody said anything. The guard took his club and knocked out the front teeth of the Mexican dude sitting in the front seat and walked off of the bus. The knees of this dude sitting in front on me were clacking together so loudly, they could hear it way in the back. Then he started crying, saying this wasn't fair; he didn't do it. This old convict stood up and said, "Quit acting like a bitch," and elbowed him in the head. "You got three damned years to do. I got fifty. You know damn well you fondled them kids, you pervert."

The last person they brought on the bus was Richard Johnson, long-time dope man. In exchange for a lesser sentence, he gave up a lot of people. He took a lot of people down—black, white, and brown, and crooked cops, so he had to be protected. His life was on the line.

In his day he was big. He is best remembered for his many friends. I heard BB talk about his mansion on a hill with a tennis court and indoor pool, his beautiful women and fancy cars. He had a doctor's degree. His mistress brought him down. He had neglected her and put his hand on her one too many times. She was with him from the jump and documented everything. She handed the police enough information to take three crews down and hit them with federal and state charges.

It was a mystical ride; we took off into the clouds like a fairy tale. We rode for three hours in the dark through the mountains and desert. There was a bathroom in the back of the bus, but it was kind of hard to use, all chained up. That's why I didn't eat a lot of breakfast. If you have to shit, you're in trouble. As dawn was breaking, you could see that we were riding through the mountains, farmland, and desert.

Aftershocks

It hits you while you are taking that long ride up north
You have just given up your rights as a free man
You have been taken out of your world
You are given a number
They take away your jewelry and your clothes
They take away your friends your family
They take away all of the good things that this world has
to offer

Place you in this new world
Give you new clothes
And give you new friends a new family
And expect you to co-exist in this new world with all of the
diverse backgrounds and all of the different personalities.

Tracy—D.V.I.

After all of that riding, we finally arrived at Tracy. One of
the old timers said they got some crazy ass youngsters in
this motha-fucka. Tracy was one of those prisons where they
liked to send the young offenders. Still in our prison whites
we were marched down a long hall way to classification.

In classification they explained the rules and the
regulations and also saw if you were compatible with the
other inmates. They had your whole file in front of them,
and they still asked you retarded questions. They ran this

wonderful program down, too, and said it works, if you work it.

Tracy had a vicious reputation for stabbings, killings, rape, and riots. Tracy was one of those places where it was difficult for you to do your time. Tracy was no joke. You could get your head cut off or get your ass hole stretched. Diamond and I were placed in the same unit in the same cell. We unpacked our stuff which wasn't much; they made us throw away a lot of stuff in Chino.

When we came out for lunch, all eyes were on us. I didn't see one familiar face. When we got to the chow hall, I saw wino Willie. I hadn't seen Willie in years. He came over and shook our hands and asked about home and told what's happening with everybody. Then he started to give us the real on Tracy. Willie told us to stay out of the bullshit and the politics, and if the brothas got into it with anybody, stay out of it.

I couldn't stand a fuckin coward. I was not staying in my cell I was gonna be right upfront because I liked that gladiator shit.

In the chow hall, the segregation was voluntary. The brothas sat with the brothas; whites with whites; brown with the brown. It was the same thing with the housing. There were cliques, groups, circles, wannabes, and supporters. Some of the men walked around with their chest out all puffed up. A lot of it was an image they needed to project. Most of them were fuckin track stars Carl Lewis couldn't catch them on his best day. They ain't gonna fight shit.

We were voluntarily placed in the kitchen. The guard unlocked our cell door at 4 a.m. We got up and washed and had to be at the kitchen by 4:30 a.m. The kitchen was big enough to feed 200 to 300 men at a time to accommodate this 3,000-man facility. The men were fed in shifts 200 at a time.

You lined up on the left side, grabbed a tray, grabbed some silverware, and walked to the serving line. There five to six men were standing on the serving line placing the food on the trays. The meals were prepared in these gigantic pots and pans that had to be cleaned after each meal. The trays and the silverware had to be washed after each meal. Thank God they had a dishwasher. The tables had to be cleaned, the floors swept, and the floors mopped after each meal.

After a month rolled by, I realized prison was a miniature replica of the world outside. We had our own schools, TV station, radio station, sports teams, jobs, stores, and laundry. We had just about every culture in there doing time. There was a lot of talent in that place. There were welders, pipe fitters, sheet metal workers, cooks, NAs, farmers, doctors, teachers, sales, construction workers, preachers, MTA'S, artists, and musicians.

White people were the most trusted so they were put in the positions of trust, and I guess you know who is the least trusted. My partner in the kitchen was this white dude name Bobby from the valley. We rode from Chino to Tracy together. Also working with us in the kitchen was this white dude named Butch who thought Bobby was a real cutie. He got real steamed up whenever he looked at Bobby.

One time Butch caught Bobby in the back of the kitchen alone and snuck up on Bobby and kissed him on the neck and said, "Hey, princess."

Bobby turned around and pushed Butch away and asked him, "What's wrong with you?"

Butch pinned Bobby down and was about to put the chokehold on him. I heard the noise and walked to the back of the kitchen. I saw Butch on top of Bobby. I snatched him off of Bobby. Butch got up and ran back into the kitchen.

I told Bobby, "You are gonna have to do something to him. He's not gonna stop trying to fuck you." Ferocious had a nice talk

With Butch and he never said anything else to Bobby. We didn't get caught up in all the hate, people were people Bobby had blue eyes and and blonde hair and we pulled off of the same joint and swigged off of the same whiskey bottle that was our friend and dare you to touch him. Bobby paroled 3 months later he sent us money and pictures.I got a letter from Bobby's sister three months later with his obituary he got killed in a motor cycle accident

TRACY THE REAL

We were coming back from dinner, when I saw my first 187.

This dude was at the game table playing cards, and these three dudes tipped up on him and carved him up. He looked like Swiss cheese when they were done with him.

A week later this dude was in his cell taking a deep squat on his toilet, and these dudes stepped into his cell and busted his heart. I realized right away they were not jokin'; they were playing for keeps.

THE PRISON SYSTEM

When I entered the prison system, the African American population was still under the influence of the Civil Rights Movement and the Panther Party. Teaching and re-directing lives was available. Their goal was to prepare the next generation to take the torch.

Some of these brothas took us up under their wings and prepared us. They knew we had to carry the load, keep the fire going; someone did that for them and because they were done there.

Most of the men that took us up under their wings were lifers, possibly never getting out. What they did for us was to take their wisdom, knowledge, and spirit and pour it into us, in hopes that we would pass it onto others and when we hit the streets we would impact the lives of others.

I knew it was wild up there. I just didn't know these motha-fuckas up there were retarded.

SUDAN A

We were on the iron pile the first time we met Sudan. There were all kinds of rumors circulating the joint about him and what he stood for. We started off talking about the Lakers, and we began to get into the deep stuff, the real on that place.

Sudan told me there were rumors circulating around about me, also. He knew that a lot of the men there couldn't stand me, and they knew I was a Bounty Hunter out of Nickerson Gardens. "The other brothers say you did done pretty foul shit out there on the streets."

Sudan said, "I ain't mad at you, because we all done stupid things and made bad decisions when we were young. We all started off as something else." Then he asked me, "What are you gonna do with the rest of your time?"

I thought about it.

Then he said, "Are you willing to put something different in it?"

I thought about it.

Then he went deep on us again.

That evening in the chow hall I tried to sit at the table with Sudan, Big Duty, and Jespah. They told me I couldn't sit at the table with them because I didn't have any notches. I had to sit at the table with the other criminals.

Then he began to teach the twelve years he had been in the joint. He used the time wisely; he invested it in himself so that he could help others. He reminded me of what is important. What he said lit a fire in me, a light came on.

SUDAN

Sudan was one of those hard-core militant brothers from the

Panther Party Era that the guards couldn't stand. He spoke my kind language. His message to the brothers of this generation was to stop fighting each other; stop crossing each other; stop passing on old grudges and old beefs.

Just like on the streets, a lot of the brothers weren't hearing the message. He was trying to connect with other brothers that felt like him, the jungle brothers. They wanted to continue to operate in the confusion. That same selfishness and division that had us fucked up on the streets, had us fucked up in there.

I didn't see it, but he walked to the infirmary later. The first time I saw a brother being stabbed up by this hate group. It messed me up. I couldn't understand it. The thing that really made me mad was there were seven or eight Negroes sitting at the game tables watching this brother being attacked. They were hiding up under the tables, running like girls. These three haters stabbed him up real good. Even though he was an old bitch ass nigga, instead of hollering for help and trying to hide, he should have been slugging it out.

I knew when we came off lockdown a week later, it was gonna be some shit. I wanted to be right in the middle of it. This was my second week there. Sudan said it wasn't my time yet.

"What do you mean it isn't my time yet?" I asked him.

"They will handle it," he said. "You will be part of the second wave to deal with the Repocussion."

I said, "Ah, fuck that . . ."

Before I could finish what I was saying, Sudan gave this signal, unleashing the dog. I heard a yell. Big Dookie threw this white boy off of the tier and his ass splatters right in front of us. I jumped up and said, "Oh, shit, this is what I've been waiting on." Then I moved in closer so I could get a better look. I saw this white dude get gutted. I grabbed my stool.

Sudan called me; I ignored his ass, but it was too late. I hit one of them so hard I broke the stool over his head. I picked up one of the broken legs of the stool and moved Jespah out of the way. I beat the shit out of that one stool leg.

They shot so much gas in there, it was like fog. You couldn't see nothing with your eyes watering. I looked in the corner and saw these big muscular Negroes all huddled in the corner shaking, supposed to be bad ass bangers. Two of them were in the television room saying they couldn't wait for some shit to kick off.

Jespah saw them hiding, too. "I see what kind party this is," Jespah said. "We are gonna have to pass out some panties around this motha-fucka joint because it is full of ho's, bitch-ass motha-fuckas."

When all was said and done, three of them had to be wheeled out on gurneys.

Sudan looked at me and said, "You're kind of hard-headed, ain't you?" I said, "Absolutely." At dinner that evening the others asked Sudan 'who is that youngster that got down with us'? did you see that youngster get down ? the youngster from the head hunters.

THE BROTHAS

A lot of young men, when they enter the prison, enter the system scared. If you are the kind of man that doesn't fight, turn your back on violence. The rumors you hear about the prison system in county jail will scare you. They are uncertain. and don't want to fight and don't want to deal with all of the confusion, especially the weaker brothas. They join the church or the Muslims in hopes of doin' their time in peace. Those that are dirty do it to get up under some protection until they sort things out. The Muslims protect their own, fight to the last man if they have to, and I don't mean none of this in a disrespectful way. It is just how it is. I have to say this: the Nation of Islam has turned a lot of brothas around.

AFTER

After coming into the knowledge of our struggle as people presented the way they presented it to me I was overwhelmed. It changed everything I believed in and the way I believed in everything. I felt like a fucking traitor, doing drive-by's, walk-by's, jumping on brothers out of jealousy, selling poison. Sudan told me change begins in the mind and the heart. We wanted to make a difference and we stepped up. I had something to prove anyway.

I was from Nickerson Gardens and the three brothers that came here from the bricks before me made us look bad, tarnished our image our rep.; they weren't Hunters. I didn't like the way they represented us. I won't tell you how they embarrassed us but they disgraced us. I had work to do.

INNOCENT

I think the one thing about bangin' that disturbs me the most and keeps me up some nights is the innocent lives that are taken. The accidental shootings and initiation bullshit and the pure hate and revenge shit. I have done drive-bys, walk-bys, but I have never shot into a crowd where there were women or children, never. I didn't think about that at the time, but what I did was wrong and will always be wrong.

Many lives are destroyed when you pick up the gun: the victim's family and the trigger man and his family. The young man that pulled the trigger doesn't know but his life will never be the same; that incident will always haunt him. There will never be a day that goes by when he doesn't think about it. It is a painful memory that doesn't go away. Somethings you can't bury deep enough. When the prison system is done with him, when he leaves, he will be all fucked with issues, a whole new set of problems. Probably come back to the joint a few more times if he doesn't OD or get killed out there. I saw it every day. Where were all the big trigger pullers now? You ruin your life and you destroy their's

At home is a mother that misses her child, her son, her daughter and a sister that misses her brother and a brother that misses his sister. The victim's family will never stop grieving that loss every birthday, holiday, anniversary of the shooting. It just goes on. There is no straitening it out there is no going back and doing it again. Don't throw your life away

Choose life and live.

CHARACTERS

One of the things that will keep you in trouble is gambling. The men expect to be paid and paid in full on time or you put them in a position where they had to do something to you. This dude called his self Fast Black Eddie, player, pimp, gambler. When he got there he had this long perm down to his shoulder. When Ferocious winked at him he immediately went to the barber and cut that shit off.

Eddie gambled one night and lost $1,000.00 to Stoney. He didn't know at the time he was being triple-teamed. They gave him a deadline to pay it off and he missed it; he had to the end of the day to get it done or tonight could his last night on this planet. Eddie usually came out of cell for recreation in the evening. What Eddie did was to stay in, take all of his cosmetics out of the containers, and fill the cosmetic containers with water. Then he took a big brown grocery bag, put balled up newspaper in it, and stuffed the empty cookie and cracker boxes with newspaper and put five soups on top of the bag. Then he cut newspaper down to the size of ducats (prison money) and put ducats on the bottom and the top of the stack to make look like fifty ducats.

When the final lockdown bell sounded off, P and Stoney were on their way up to his cell and they were strapped. Eddie came out of his cell and walked down to their cell and showed them the goodies. He was stalling. He was holding onto the bag until they stepped inside their cell. Stoney and P were slapping hands, saying they were gonna eat good that tonight and deep down inside Eddie was laughing, too. They finally stepped inside of their cell and Eddie took the ducats and dropped them inside the grocery bag and handed them the bag. The guards locked them down for the night. The next morning P and Stoney ran down to

Eddie's cell. Eddie's punk ass locked it up or was taken into protective custody.

JIMBO

Jimbo was one of those brothas from the South that ain't gonna be without a ho. Steve was the dude Jimbo beat on and beat and turned out in the county jail. Steve was also married and the father of two children. Around Tracy, Steve was called Sugar; most people didn't know that his name was Steve.

A jailhouse ho is another name for a slave. Sugar turned tricks for Steve, and it was also Sugar's job to iron Jimbo's clothes, hand wash his shorts and T-shirts and hang them up, and on his knees scrub Jimbo's floor and his toilet.

Today Sugar had a visit. His wife and two children traveled from central California to come and see him. Sugar was excited but he was worried about the other men exposing him. Sugar was on his way to his visit, and Jimbo jammed him up and told him to go back in his cell and shave the hair from around his mouth because "you ain't no man, motha-fucka. You're a ho and always will be. Take that shirt from out of them pants and tie it up around your waist like a bitch."

Sugar proceeded to his visit, got down the hall way and took the shirt from around his waist, and tucked it into his pants. He stuck his chest out and walked into the visiting room like he was the hardest nigga in the joint. Those that know him had a grin on their face but they didn't expose his.

Red Dog ain't gonna let it slide. As soon as his visit was over, he went over to Sugar's table. He said to Sugar's wife, "Why you with this bitch-ass nigga? He has been with more men than you have."

Steve put his head down for a moment and turned red, and then he held his head up and said, "Why you trippin', man? Jealous? You ain't got nobody."

Red Dog balled his fist up and Stevie balled his fist up and said, "I dare you." The guard stepped in and made Red Dog leave the visiting room.

Jimbo got a visit. His parents were there, but he forgot all about his parents and went straight to Sugar's table and introduced himself and starts in. Jimbo humiliated him in front of his wife and children. Sugar puts his head down and went on quiet; he knew Jimbo would break his neck if he crossed the line.

Sugar's wife looked at him and said, "They call you Sugar and you are up here getting fucked in the ass and sucking dicks. What am I supposed to tell your children, you fuckin' fag?"

They got into a loud, heated discussion and she hit him. The guard terminated his visit. Jimbo tried to rap to her. She said, "If you're fucking him, then there is something wrong with you, too."

Sugar took a hand full pills and tried to leave this planet but he was unsuccessful he was transferred.

Grandpa was a young old man. He would say when he saw us. I loved to see them niggas walking down the hallway. No one did it better when we came down the hallway. The inmates got a show.

ONCE

Once a month, the general population is treated to a movie. Nothing fancy, nothing new. We had our own movie theater.

Today a young man was stabbed to death while the movie was being shown. He was set up from the beginning. He didn't know his time was up sitting next to his assassins. The dude on the left held down his left arm, the dude on the right held down his right arm. The dude sitting directly behind him put the locks down on his head and his mouth while the dude next to him pulled out a sword and busted his heart. They propped him up in his seat and all quietly moved away.

NAMES

Names and nicknames say a lot about a person, who you are and what you do for a living, what you think, and what your fantasies are. There was Outlaw Bob, Redneck Bob, Tattoo Bob, Dope Fiend Bob, Biker Bob, Long Asshole Bob, Shit Ka Bob, Cowboy Bob, Witch Doctor Bob, Chicken

Shit Ass Bob, No Shower-taking Dope Fiend No Teeth Alcoholic Bob, Ear Bob (someone bit this dude's ear off in the county jail), It Ka Bob (they also called him Monster, Frankenstein), Sheep-, Chicken—and Steer-fuckin' Bob.

Then there were the Dogs: Mad Dog, Cotton Dog, Sheep Dog, Red Dog, Black Dog, Under Dog, Top Dog, Big Dog, Bull Dog, and Straw Dog,

The Jacks were: Mad Jack, Black Jack, One Eye Jack, Tip Toe Jack, Jacking Jack, Jamaican Jack, Automatic Jack, Flap Jack, Pop Lockin' Jack, Cracker Jack, Smack Water Jack, Box Head Jack, and Jack from Hell, the Devil.

The pimps and the players had names like: Miracle, Ice Water Johnson, Sweet, Comfort, Treasure, Destiny, Pimp Daddy Taylor, Mac Daddy Mike, Justice, Black diamond and Onyx were from dirty pussy California.

Then we had the gangsters and bangers they carried the name of every well-known mobster you could think of. Aside from those, there was Big Money, Bank Roll, Dollar Bill, and Cash Money.

THE STAND

With all of the brothers we looked to for leadership and direction on lockdown or in the security housing unit snatched up during raids and the last series of hits, there was some uncertainty in the air. The brothers that didn't fight or refused to fight might have had to break a nail, sweat out them perms, and do something besides walking the yard and running their mouth. I just didn't understand how you go from kicking ass all over your neighborhood and blasting people to hiding in your cell like girls.

Mousie was one of them Crips that hated me back in the day. He and other Crips wanted to jump me in Juvi years ago. The Crips had me surrounded 50 to 1. It was a good thing to have Crip cousins. He ended it real quickly. As Mousie was leaving he said one day, "I am not gonna have my cousin to protect me, and it is gonna be me and him." I would have snapped his ass in two

He was a little fella; I don't think Mousie came to my chest but he had a big heart and a lot of mouth. He saw how dysfunctional we were as a people in some areas of our lives and the Negro mentality some of the brothers had in here. He and Bones came to me one evening and offered their services. We smoked from the peace pipe and have been boys ever since. Little by little we began to build on that momentum; more brothers began to cross over.

CHAPTER 8
JoHNNY BAd Ass

BANGIN' THE DEF

It doesn't take any heart to do a drive; any body can shoot an unarmed person; anybody can be brave when you got your homeboys standing behind you; anybody can be brave after a couple of forties and a couple of joints. Anybody can be brave when you have one group outnumbered 3 to 1 or 2 to 1.

Banging is when the enemy is strapped and you and your boys got your shit and you go out there knowing that you are gonna get blasted by the guards and there are tons of tear gas, knives, fists, stun guns, and pipes flying at you; that's bangin'. Sniping at people isn't bangin neither is shooting unarmed people. In here we get to see what you can do without your guns and your boys.

THE GET DOWN

Moses, he didn't have any friends there in Tracy; he hung out solo. If you spoke to him he would speak back or just nod his head. When he was a kid down South, he was burned badly from his chin to his toes. The ignorant brothas used to call him names like Monster Man, Scarecrow behind his back.

One afternoon I was working in the kitchen. Moses was in there and we began to talk. Moses said he hadn't heard nothing but bad things about us; nothing but dirty dirt. Later on he joined us on the yard. He talked non-stop. Unbelievable; it was like he was holding it in for years. I told him we couldn't call him Moses; that was too plain. Ferocious said, "He's dirty; that nigga is dirty I mean it." I said, "Dirty, it is." No more weed either he's like a dam vacuum cleaner.

I was smuggling knives through Tracy so we would be armed. This fool intercepted the last shipment and turned around and sold it to the enemy for some drugs and didn't think we were gonna find about it. You don't like to but sometimes you have to destroy your own. We were gonna fuck them up anyway all that did was to make us speed up our plans. They were planning to move on the brothas soon, not us, the bitch ass niggas that don't fight and run.

Seven of the bastards that had to go were in our wing and there were four more across the hall. When we tear into that ass here they will be rocking across the hallway.

Steel is best served when it is serve cold in the morning. I got Big Duty, Diamond, Dirty, Frisco Mike, Mousie, Bones and Mad Mark. It ain't about color; those bastards had to go because of what they stood for. The brothas knew not to touch any of the other whites unless they got in the way.

When I came out for breakfast, I put extra cloths and a towel in the shower. We wanted to clean house before we went. That Negro that sold our knives was asleep in his cell. He didn't hear the two brothas step inside his cell. He was asleep with the blanket over his head. They lit his ass up like a Xmas tree and rolled him up in his blanket and put him under his bed. Two of the men that came back from breakfast was standing on the first tier under had a few drops of blood hit them on the shoe and they looked and moved quietly away.

When we came back from breakfast I told Dirty, "Close the gate." I pulled out my knife and walked up to that no-shower taking ass Pinky and I ran his ass through. He screamed like a girl and I hit his ass in the throat and he dropped to the ground. I stepped to the next piece of shit, Fish. He and his other white friends were jumping on brothas in—County Jail. I decorated his ass, too. Big Duty hit Fat Rat so hard through the stomach I saw the front part of the blade sticking out of his back. Mad Mark must have special-ordered it; it looked like a spear. He was chasing Bitch Ass-looking Bobby and Bobby was running for his life.

Somebody Bobby tripped up, and I got his ass. I hit his ass so hard I couldn't pull the knife out of him.

I didn't have a knife now, so it was time to start throwing motha-fuckas off the tier. We got one more bastard that had to go. I caught him on the second tier trying to hide, and I socked his ass and picked him up and tried to throw him off the tier. He was holding on, and I kicked his ass in the face. He fell down to the first tier. Dirty's job was to shortstop any interference, and this white dude crossed the line. Dirty lit his ass up. There were bodies laid out all over the tier; blood everywhere; and blood all over me.

I was getting in the shower when the guards storm troop the place. I was in my shorts, and the guards told me to get up against the wall. This white dude walked up to the guards and said, "It was that black bastard right there," talking about me, "and them black motha-fuckas right there."

They haul us all off to the lockup unit. The lockup unit is the jail within the jail where they keep the bad boys that can't keep their hands or knives to themselves.

The next morning I was coming back from the hearing on the charges against me. As I walked by this white dude cell he threw piss on me and called me a nigger. I was handcuffed so there wasn't nothing I could do about it, when I came out to shower that evening I saw that he slept with his head to the bars. His hair was real long, touching the floor. I asked Kidogo for some newspaper. I rolled the newspaper up and used it to fish a grip of his hair. I grabbed his hair and snatched his ass out of that bed and to the bars and I hit his ass twice with my pencil. I fucked him up. The guards cuffed me and put me in the back in the isolation cells. These cells have nothing in them so I guessed I would be singing and doing push ups for the next ten days.

Two days later I got some company next door, Johnny Walker Red from Louisiana. He got into it with the white boys. We talked all day about L.A., women, sports and the system. The next morning I came out to shower. I was looking for the brotha I was talking to last night. I saw this little white man. I said, "Where's Johnny?" He said, "I'm right here." I said, "Damn, a white boy!" He talked and moved like a nigga. That's why he was fighting with the white boys they don't play that shit.

There was no room for us upstairs and after ten days they had to move us out of the isolation cells into the regular locked cells. They moved me a few cells from the piss thrower. I was not done with him yet. He had to have a few stitches from pencil stabbing, bitch. I had been saving up shit for two days I have it in a bread bag. It's real ripe. I walked down to his cell. He likes to sleep with his mouth open. I hit him right across the mouth and nose. He screamed like a girl. That's right I threw shit. They put me back in isolation for another ten days. They can put me under this motha-fucka as long as they let me out when it is time to go home.

BOOKS

The man with the book cart came by one afternoon. He came by about once every two weeks. I was bored. Sitting in a cell twenty-three hours a day gets to you. For a while I was really going through it. I was looking at the different books on his cart. I asked to read this book called *Oliver Twist* by Charles Dickens. I started reading it after dinner, and I remember the stories my English teachers Mrs. Dancy and Mr. Higgins use to read to us at Markham, how they made the stories come to life and their words come back to remembrance. I couldn't put it down. Reading became part of my daily rutine

Then I began to look for other books by Charles Dickens. I went from that to the *Pirates of the Caribbean*, *The Three Musketeers*, and *Uncle Tom's Cabin*. What it did was open up and my creative imagination. I began to visualize each passage in my head, using my creative imagination, and the books came to life.

THE LOCK-UP UNIT

When we were in the lockup unit back in the day it was a war zone. Bombs were going off and being tossed into people's cells. Zip guns were being fired at people packed with scrap metal, pepper, and salt. People swiping at other people with swords as you walk the tier. You had to be on your toes as you walked the tier or you might get stuck with a pole. People were being fire-bombed in their cells. I saw a dude's bed go up in smoke; by the time the guards put out the fire and pulled him out of that cell he looked like a piece of bacon.

Sometimes these cell doors mysteriously popped open, letting your enemy out on you,in the middle of hell broke loose. I was 19 years old I had never seen no shit like that.

DIAGNOSTIC STUDY ONE

Next month I appear before the board in the prison system at that time if you were in prison for a violent crime you were sent to specialist to be evaluated there are only 2 prisons set up for something like this.Where they are sending me, I know this prison is full of homosexuals the aggressive kind and men with mental problems.I am doing this in hopes of getting out sooner or getting some of this time sliced in half.They cross the line I am gonna do what I have to do.Don't touch me and don't ask me shit.

I roll up my personal property and I am chained up and loaded on the goose there are a few people on the bus already.Three hours later when we reach our destination some of these dudes on the bus eyes light up. All of the bitch comes out.

We are all unloaded off of the bus and marched down this long hall way still chained up.As I am walking in I see long hair.dresses, wigs and I smell a lot of perfume. These men are in dresses and wigs, make up are smiling and waving at you. This big one about 6'6 300 pounds smiles at me and say 'hi little daddy.

He must be new at this his wig is all twisted wrong, lipstick in the wrong place, he must be a Ho in training. Some of the men come to jail and get that bitch switch flipped on. They start off desiring and touching other men. He starts playing in one of them ass and they eventually get around to playing in his. The next time you see them they look like girls wigs, makeup, tight pants, switchin. They call the homosexuals queens in the jail system. These homosexuals down there they didn't cut you no slack they are persistent. They tried to buy your time, negotiate dick deals with you; some queens as they are called didn't have a problem paying for it. Some fools didn't have a problem selling it; they were used to being taken care of by women. The queens would give them drugs, money, clothes, cook and clean up for you and behind you. They would do anything to keep you there with them. This attracted a lot of men to this type of environment, easy time and an opportunity to lay up with other men.

The first thing I wanted to do was to take a shower but I couldn't do that because they were on wee-wee watch. I took my shirt off and saw about four or five pull their heads back from around the corner. They wanted to get a show today.

My boy Mac Daddy Mike was up there. If there was some pimpin' and playing and gambling going on, I knew he was right in the middle of it. I walked over to his wing and to the cell he was in. He wasn't there. I could see that his cell was laid out, decorated with carpet, paintings, television, radios, tennis cloths hung up neatly. Stacks of soups, zoos-zoos and wams-wams. I asked about MD, and they told me that he was on the yard. I walked up on him and MD had his ho's at attention giving them their instructions for the day. He felt my presence and looked around. His mouth dropped to the floor; he could not believe what he saw. He gave me a homeboy hug. We talked about everything, how I ended up in the system, and how he ended up in there.

MD tried to talk me into staying there, but I told him straight out I ain't with all this funny bunny shit that was going on in there. Then I told him I asked to be sent back to Tracy immediately. Then he asked me why I would go back to all that crazy shit. I told him because I liked that gladiator shit; I liked it. Then he looked me in the eyes and said, "We can get paid and stay high every day; get our dicks sucked regularly run this motha—fucka."

I said, "MD, I ain't into that shit. I can't do it. I have to be around some real niggas. I would have to hurt one these motha-fuckas to stress a point."

DIAGNOSTIC STUDY TWO

I was riding solo. You couldn't trust nobody; some of the men there ain't what they said they were. Some of them were down there for different reasons; some of them had been hit or had hits out on them; and some of them were there to get their asshole tickled and love on them some men.

I don't know what you know about them but they pursued real men. They would just find a seat in the area where you were and just lust off you. They would have this look in their eyes; it wasn't a "hi, homeboy" look. You didn't know if they were thinking about fucking you or dreaming about you fucking them. They talked kind of loud and you heard the names they called each other, names like: Sugar, Love, Christy Love, Candy, Easter Bunny, Moist Mike, Pony Boy and Butt Weak. That one Butt Weak, I think, was the one that had been writing me all of the retarded letters and leaving gifts by my cell door. Those dudes there get real dick sick.

The next day I was on my way to iron pile. As I looked across the field I saw a party or a co-ed going on, music with dancing. I saw about twenty homosexuals over there dancing. What was tripping me out was seeing two hard-core bangers with their hands in the air over there dancing with them other men. They were over there breaking it down to. They looked over and saw me and flagged me to come over and join them. I said, "Hell, no." I left but I did stick around to see if the bangers were gonna slow dance with them, too. Times ain't gonna ever be that damn hard or desperate to where I'm gonna dance with another damn man.

Later on when the bangers caught themselves, they hunted me down and put the beg on me. They said they were high and got caught up. They said to me, "Please don't tell anybody that we were over there dancing with them other men," and they said, "Yeah, nobody. That will mess up my rep." They handed me two joints and we had a deal. This Muslim brotha that was in Tracy with us arrived today. I told him, 'these homosexuals were serious about getting theirs'. These two dudes were sitting behind us I heard the little one ask the big one could he play with it. The Muslim brotha heard it to he couldn't believe he said Sodom and Gomorah.

DIAGNOSTIC STUDY

Day three: I was on the iron pile working out and this dude approached me. He had his thumb in his mouth and his other hand playing with his ear. I knew he was fucked up when I saw him. He walked up to me and before he could get anything out, I said, "Don't ask me, shit. Beat it."

That fat motha-fucka started crying and he left. He came back with a guard and told the guard I threatened his life. I looked at him and he went and stood behind the guard. Then he said to me, "You told me you loved me." I said, "I ain't told you no shit like that." Then the guard walked away and his ass ran away.

The next day he came around me again harassing me with his thumb and his ear. I looked around and made sure no one was looking. I slapped his ass down to the ground, and he got up and ran. That's how you break that shit up. I never had a problem out of him again. He wasn't that damn retarded; he knew how to molest little boys. He was lucky that was all I did.

I was on my way back to my cell, and I caught this dude sliding a letter up under my cell door. I told him, "You are the one that has been sending me all them fucked up freaky ass letters, a dam runt?" I tried to tell him in a calm manner, "I don't like men and stop sending letters or fucking else."

Then he said, "I can't help it. I love you."

I said, "Shit, what's wrong with you?" Then I realized he was fucked up, too. I had to tell him, "If I catch you anywhere around my cell door, I am gonna put your ass to sleep."

I went to the office and checked on my transfer. They said maybe in a few days.

DIAGNOSTIC STUDY 3

Some of the men there acted like they were deeply in love with these other men.They walked around all hugged up with each other, holding hands and kissing. They kissed each other when they first saw each other in the morning, and they gave each other a smack on the lips before the final lockdown at night. The men in there got real jealous if they saw you staring at their guy-girl. I just stayed the fuck away. They even marry each other in a broom jumping ceremony. I was still getting retarded letters from other men. The last one said, "Quit getting all uptight and being anti-social; relax and open your mind and let go. You will find that this is a wonderful place to do your time." The last thing he said was, "Only a man really knows how to really love another man."

I said to myself 'they got it all twisted?' This was the kind of stuff you had to put up with in there, all jokes aside. I just wanted to get back to Tracy.

I was sent back to Tracy four days later. I did an eighteen-month term in lockup, and they let me and the rest back in the general population. They told me to behave myself, and I assured that I would. I got a job working back in the kitchen. Two weeks later I got my old job back in the kitchen. The old dude that had had it went to Chino.

I got a letter. Roy and Angel just got out of lockup for the same shit. Me and Diamond were hanging tough; Those eighteen months in the hole were ruff on him; his ass was three shades lighter. Roy sent me some pictures of him and some of the other homies.

I got a letter from this girl name Karen today. She let me know it was time for her to move on. She said she met somebody she wanted to be with. I understood. I just wished I could have gotten a farewell shot. I took it one day at a time or day by day; I didn't mark the days. I didn't have a calendar and didn't want one. I tried to lose track of days, years, months. I just wanted them to let me know when it was time for me to go home. Most of my thoughts at that point were futuristic, very seldom did I focus on this dungeon. I was somewhere else always. I went through all that shit for nothing harassed by other men the board said 'see you in about 6 years. "

PRESSURING

The guards and other institutions liked to use the term pressuring to describe the heat put on the softies by the bullies and the ass pirates. If you didn't know, it was against the law in there to fuck somebody that didn't want to be fucked. A lot of the men that got turned out brought some of that shit on themselves, running around in some 'come, fuck me's,' hair down to their back, and tight pants, getting those men all worked up. And not fighting back, you protect the sacred circle at all cost.

Some of the men weren't ever getting out and some had another twenty to thirty years to go before they would see daylight. This was the closest thing they would see for a long time to the real thing, and some of them weren't gonna go without or be without a ho'. And they dropped the hammer.

There was more control over it in there than there was in the county jail where anything goes. A lot of the stories that are passed onto the public like ass locks, butt plugs or fucked or be fucked that's television.

Ass Pirates

When Eddie and Ferocious hit Tracy, everything changed. They took knocking other men in the head and taking their ass on another level. Their philosophy was "too many bitch ass motha-fuckas around here to be beating your shit every night. They were in the bitch making business." Bernard Williams was also known as Saint Bernard as in holy. I met Ferocious in the county jail through Angel; Ferocious was like Angel practically raised by the State of California.

When Bernard was five years old, his mother took him out for some ice cream and told him to sit at the bus stop and eat. She had to go back into the store and get something she forgot. She never came back for him, and at the age of five he entered the foster system. He went from place to place for years, too many to count and to remember. There was abuse, neglect, molesting of other children; he had a lot of horror stories. He ran away at the age of ten. To survive on the streets, he and two friends committed robberies. He went to camp, then Youth Authority, and then prison on robberies.

His ass-taking partner was Eddie. Both of Eddie's parents were school teachers. Eddie came from a good home. Eddie got A's and B's in school and was on his way to college until he started hanging out on the east side. After that all he wanted to do was to low ride and chase car freaks and get high.

I didn't understand why they did what they did. He told me basically what P had told me. It ain't nothing wrong with a little boy once in awhile as long as I am the fucker and not the fuck—ee

How they went about there business was brutal in the beginning they worked together as a team.Ferocious would follow his victum back to their cell from the shower and tell them to drop that towel get your ass in position and spread them donuts. Some of them resisted and that cell would hum for a few minutes. Ten minutes later Ferocious come down stairs fixing his pants back up sometimes singing. He would put his own twist on a James Brown classic' so good,so good cause I fucked you.

Eddie was a maniac he would carry around an assortment of nude pictures around with him. Eddie would step in the victims cell beat them half to death then tape a nude photo on back of their head and ride them. Eddie told them I don't mine getting it dead or alive I'm gonna fuck.

Some of the men after they were assaulted would limp up Front leaking, bleeding some of them would have to be stitched up and tell the guard what happened.He told the guard this black dude step inside his cell knocked him in head and flipped him on his stomach ripped his pants off then wham—o right up the ol ca-zoo. Sometimes the men that were sexually assaulted would commit suicide or try to kill themselves, it ruined them

ME

Loving on another fuckin man that ain't gonna happen. Me, I was on stroke status. Ain't nothing another man could do for me.

This is the one place where cock fights and sword fighting is legal. Masturbation has all kinds of names in there: slappin' the salami, choking the chicken, five knucko chucko, and my favorite: doin' the jerk.

I remember the first time I was trying to get my stroke on I was hesitant because I knew you shouldn't be toying with yourself like that. Deacon Williams told us a hand would reach down from heaven and smack me on the hands and say 'cut that shit out.'

Over the years you develop all kinds of ways of getting it done, techniques. The mind is a remarkable thing; it is like a computer. It allows you to file away all these memories. You can pull them down when you need them. All you have to do is to add your creative imagination with it or to it. The mind can bring back to remembrance of those special moments and place you right back in that motel room with her. You remember what she looked like, what she had on, them legs, them titties, how good the sex was. You have all that shit going on in your mind at the same time while you are trying to hold all these thoughts. All you are doing is re-fucking all of your memories. How often did I do that? As much as I needed to. I am sure that I have set all kind of Olympic records in the sprints and the long distance events. The only thing you worried about was permanently bruising, putting a bad bow on your shit and sanding your shit down to nothing.

VABOOM

Sometimes you need a distraction from this place. Everything is routine for the sake of sanity you have to switch it up.

I got high when I could smoke me a fat one or drink when it was available. Vaboom, the two years I have been here, he has been entertaining the hell out of the other prisoners. He believes that was the gift that God gave him: entertaining people. He would get requests to do Richard Pryor and Rudy Ray Moore, and do them well. What everyone really liked were the stories he told. He would tell these death-defying stories of espionage, drug deals of him rescuing POWs, rescuing cruise ships from terrorists, and wiping out enemy units with his bare hands; and of course he got all of the girls. He knew the spotlight was on him, and he loved it. They didn't call him Vaboom for nothing he was a human P.A. system. The men would gather around the game tables, get their snacks, and listen. The guards even tune in.

As time went by, I found myself changing with it, growing up. I saw the world in a different light. The elders opened my eyes to a lot in the lockup unit. The elders taught me things that I should have heard from my father.

There was this quiet fire in me that burned day and night and all these dogs were doing was fueling it. The key to survival was adaptability, how well you adjusted to any condition you might have to live under in there. The real you doesn't come out until your back is against the wall. That's when you find out what you are made of.

Why we can't settle disputes with fists instead of knives is because some men only get the message in a near-death experience. Some Negroes make you want to tear off their head. This old addict was getting in the way of production, holding our people up from doing their thing. He was asked nicely to mind his own business. It was like in the time of slavery, 'I'm gonna tell the masta.' They all had a price. He asked a ridiculous price to keep quiet. I didn't even send a reply because it was too late. It was a perfect night to crack somebody in their head. There was a championship fight on and the television room was jam-packed with fight fans. Smooth stepped in the shower I gave him a few minutes to get a little steamy he couldn't see that it was me approaching him.Smooth said "is that you celly, I said 'yea it's me nigga

I took this foot long pipe and I went up side his head twice wam,

Wam it sound like an aluminum bat hitting a baseball. I ditched the pipe and went in the television room they sounded the when they found him bleeding and unconscious. He wasn't the only one getting cracked tonight down hallway these two negros have to get knots on their heads to. They won't show up to fight anything else but they will try to extort the smaller and weakers brothas.

OUT OF LOCK-UP

Vaboom, Cowboy Bill, and Madison were always glad to see me when I got out of the lockup unit. They all knew I was a problem child. Cowboy Bob would say, "Johnny, you're such a crazy fucker. You got a mean streak in you a mile long."

Vaboom would say, "I wish you weren't so damn crazy." Madison would tilt his glasses and say, "Johnny where you been." It ain't nothing like being missed. They didn't understand

CHAPTER 9
THE MEN HERE

THE MIND

Jail is a cold lonely place. Even though you are surrounded by 3,000 others, you still feel that you are by yourself. It doesn't matter if the sun is out, there is still a cloud hanging over it. Some of the men give in to this spirit and fall victim to the negative ways to get through there time. Some of the men ask for medication, the heavy stuff, to be anywhere but here. Some of the men ask for sleep aids and try to sleep through this nightmare. All of that stuff has long—and short-term side effects; some of them couldn't tell what day it was. Some of the men that have lost everything; their enthusiasm for life is gone. You slip up and let these walls collapse around you, and they will have to carry you out of here in a straight jacket. You have to stay up, motivated, encouraged; this is rough but this isn't the end of the world. Sometimes you have to be an encourager. First, you have to walk with your feet firmly planted in today; yesterday is gone and everything with it.

I had a mindset to win, not to just survive. You have to be able to function in the eye of the storm. You can't let certain thoughts overtake you. They are gonna come but you don't have to let them stay there. In here you will find yourself pushing all kinds of the thoughts in and out of your mind. I know I acted like a fucking animal; sometimes we used anger as a motivating force.

In order to have balance you had to get on a set program and fill each moment of the day with some sort of activity and not detour from it. Get up every day and thank God that you made it; like it or not, feel like it or not. I prayed for my family not for myself.

Crazy Larry arrived in Tracy and he was scared. He was out there raping and robbing prostitutes. The thing about coming to jail is you never know who's waiting on you. The uncle of one of the prostitutes was there; she got cut up and raped.

The uncle approached me about Larry, because we come from the same neighborhood. I said, "He is all yours. Bust that ass. In fact, let me tell you how to do it so you don't fuck it up."

Larry approached me but I had nothing to say. When he came down to shower that night, uncle let him get in the shower and lather his face up. The uncle hit him in the throat. Larry was trying to scream for help. They lit him up. I told Bush Monkey to turn the music up, and they came out of the shower and sat in the television room. Larry took four steps out of the shower and collapsed. That nigga must have nine lives because he survived that, too.

THE SECOND TIME AROUND

They let us all back in the general population but we didn't expect to be out there very long with them dropping kites on us. Certain inmates wanted us snatched up and put back in lockup. They feared us. They had never been up against some real niggas like us. The Negroes told the other Negroes to make sure them niggas don't get a hold of any metal. Prison officials moved on information From informants, people were taken out of the general population based on information from rats. Some of the men had been telling a long time that was what made the information coming from them reliable. They were the guards' eyes and ears out there.

Don't anything surprise me anymore. I have seen men locked up I didn't think would be locked up. I have had men run I didn't think would run. I have seen straight men flip over and become ho's. I was amazed at all of the talent that was there. I have never been around so many talented people in my life, just gifted.

Flap Jack was a twenty-six—year-old black man with a way with words and wisdom beyond his years. The brothas that weren't good with words employed his services. When some of the men needed a special letter to drive home a point to the wife or girlfriend, they'd hire Flap Jack. They said some of his letters kept the long distance relationships alive. Flap guarantees a response on all first letters or money back. They paid him with joints, vols, trues, canteen and ducats.

One of the young men that Flap wrote a letter for got a visit from one young lady Flap put a letter together for. Ten minutes into the visit she knew that it wasn't him writing the letters. He fessed up and she asked to meet Flap. When he went back to the wing he gave Flap her information. And she started visiting Flap and later on Flap paroled to her.

CHURCH

In the maximum security prisons or more hardcore joints, it is really hard to hear or focus on the Word of God when there is demon activity going on around you. The church services when we were on the line were used for gang meetings, smuggling, and homosexual activity. They did not care that it was God's house that they were disrespecting. A lot of men started staying away and studying the Word on their own. Then they formed prayer circles in the prison system where men got together outside of the church to share God's Word because of the disrespect of

God's house. It was okay in the beginning, but the whites and Hispanics wouldn't be allowed to attend the circle if the African Americans were there. God always has the final word.

MIKE BIGBITCH

I never trusted him. He had his hands in a lot of shit. He was always trying to negotiate shit behind our backs for profit. I believed he had Jespah snatched off the line because he was gonna expose him. Jespah said when we got down three years ago Mike Bigbitch punked out. Bigbitch told the white boy to lie down and he pretended to stab him didn't even skin pop him. Later two people who saw the incident confirmed what Jespah said.

That night Bigbitch stayed in. He said he had some research to do. I saw him borrow about five porn magazines. That night two visitors went into his cell on him and tattooed his ass. Instead of fighting back he got up under the bed and screamed like a bitch. I told P to turn the music up; I heard a bitch screaming.

The next matter at hand was this hater who had a tattoo with a black man hanging from a tree. That was some very bold and disrespectful shit. He had other dudes around him, so everybody had to go. The same shit as last time but some of those bastards were strapped, too. The last man locked the gate. I saw the hate in their eyes, and they saw the blood in mine. When I fuck you up, it will be for all of my failures and all of my disappointments and for being here. I torn into his fuckin ass. Without going into the bloody details when we finished it looked like something out of a horror movie. It took hours to clean up the bloody mess.

I stepped to the back, busted a window, and tossed the knife and sat down. About ten o'clock that night twelve guards armed in riot gear opened my cell door and told me they needed to put cuffs me and escort me to the lockup unit. The sergeant said I should have fuckin' known.

Lock-up—the Return

In the lockup unit we spent a great deal of time in our cells. We were let out on the yard every other day for recreation. The days we didn't go to the yard, we were in our cells twenty-three hours. We were allowed about thirty minutes to a hour to stretch our legs and shower.

I got up at six every morning. The first thing I did was to get down on my knees and thank God and pray mainly for my family. I did my pushups and sit-ups, and then washed up. Breakfast was served between 6:30 and 7: 30 a.m. In the lockup unit we were fed in our cells. A tray of food was placed on our food slot. Breakfast was sometimes powdered eggs, pancakes, French toast, cracked wheat, or oat meal.

I watched the news and read. The man with the books on a cart still came around. Once you are up, you stay up for rest of the day. Sometimes these doors mysteriously pop open, with two or three of your enemies waiting on you.

Time moved real slow in the lockup unit. You did what you could to fill the moments of the day. By the time dinner rolled around, the day was a done deal; dinner is pretty much a set schedule, except for holidays. At night I grabbed my headphone. Tracy had its own radio station with its own DJ's and radio schedule. There was jazz night, country night, R&B night, oldie night, rock night.

What we really looked forward to were the comedy shows. When Mr. Richard Pryor was on, all nationalities tuned in. Mr. Pryor was big in the joint.

I received a letter from Roy; his mother lost her battle with cancer a month ago.

FREAKS

Before K-wing was converted to a lockup unit, it used to be to a regular unit. In preparing K-wing to be converted to a lockup unit, they had to remove all the shelves from all the cells. Removing the shelves left these one inch diameters in the walls. Most people used the holes in the walls to talk to their neighbors. If you were next to your enemy, you stuffed the holes with toilet paper or you might get hit with a zip gun.

I was on my way to the shower and I noticed my neighbor, this hater, extremely to close to his wall. We were taught to observe everything and know where everyone is.

He looked at me and smiled. He acted like he was trying adjust the picture on his wall. I began to step to the shower and I decided to double back to see if he was trying to blow the place up.

When I went back to his cell he was tugging, trying to pull his pee-pee out of that one-inch diameter hole in the wall. He was up probably fucking the hole in the wall and couldn't get it out, freaky bastard. He tried to shoo me away, then he told me to keep on the low.

The brothas asked me what was wrong. I told them, "Bad ass Drew is fucking the hole in the wall." The white boy next door to him stuck his mirror around to see for himself and he told the other whites on the tier that the sick bastard was stuck in the wall. The guards told me us to lock it up and go into our cells, so they could come down the tier and see what's going on.

Four guards came down the tier and looked inside Drew's cell. The sergeant looked at Drew and said, "You know I'm gonna have to have you evaluated. I have seen some strange shit in my twenty-five years. I have never seen anybody fuck a wall."

The doctor came and gave him a shot, and they escort his freaky ass off the tier.

KEEP IN MIND

Some of the white boys liked to nigga talk. They thought because they were locked down they were safe. They had been hit with poles, bombed, and fire-bombed. When we came off of lockdown, we busted that ass on the yard. Some of the brothas didn't agree with me. They hated it when they heard I was put on this tier. When we came out to the yard after being on lockdown, it was on. I was waiting for the guard in the gun tower to go to the bathroom after his second cup of coffee. Some of the Hispanics were on the yard. If they got in the way of our attack they would get it, too.

When the guards went to the bathroom, it was on. We attacked and lit them up, and when the Hispanics came to help them, they got lit up, too. I didn't get it they talked about them the same way they talk about us. It was not about color. The guards started blasting. Then it became battleground, and it was real bad piss-and-shit fights all summer some of them. Call a truce on that shit; save it for the yard.

JOSIA

The guards brought in this black biker name Josia late one night. The brothers jumped him on the line. They said he was twisted. Big Duty hollered over at Josia, greeted him and called him "my brother."

Josia told Duty, "Mom had Jeremiah, Joshua and me. I don't remember any of you other niggas sitting at our dinner table. I ain't your brother."

Josia was a black biker that rode with a white bikers, and they abandoned his ass in there, pushed him away. I saw that he was going through withdrawals, and I got a cigarette from one of the brothers and gave it to him. We began to talk. He straight out told me, "I don't like black people. I can't stand them." He grew up in an all-white community and went to all-white schools, had all-white friends, all-white girlfriends. Somewhere in all of that he began to think he was something different. I had to warn him, "Anyway these white boys on this tier are nigga haters and they will lure and use you, and you will end up hurt."

He ignored me and asked the prison administration if he could go to the yard with the white prisoners instead of the blacks. They said no. He decided that he wouldn't go to the yard at all rather than be on the yard with us.

We were hoping that as time went along he would change. That was not the case. He was real loud and vocal about how he felt about black people. The last straw during the beauty pageant he cheered for all the white girls and booed all the sistas, calling them some ugly, big nose bitches.

Two days later I offered him another cigarette. When he reached for it, I dropped it inside his cell. After he picked the cigarette up and stood straight up, I reached inside his cell and grabbed him by his pants. I held him up to the bars where he couldn't run or move. Big Duty stabbed him through the bars and hit him again and again; Josia's knees began to buckle from the blows. He lost a lot of blood. Then I got him and he fell on the floor in his cell. The alarm went off. I got rid of the knife. I went to my cell and prepared for isolation. They cuffed me and Duty and we were escorted off the tier.

The sergeant told me, "Johnny, I am really tired of your fuckin' ass." It was back to singing the best of Motown and they threw the Bible in there with me this time.

VALENTINO

They moved this brotha that called his self Valentino next to me. When he came back from the shower he had his shirt off, and I could see his 'pimp or die' tattoo. So I saw we had a young pimp daddy on the tier. Valentino came up to me later and said, "Where I know you from, bra? Didn't you have a spot on such and such a street with about four or five ho's and drove this black caddy?"

I said, "No, never."

Then he began to badger me. "You ain't never did no pimpin'? Man, you look like a pimp."

Then Jespah jumped in, "That's what I thought you were when I first met you, Johnny Long Sausage, Pimp Daddy Blair. Then Ferocious jumped in: "I thought you was a player when I first met you, too. You act like one.

Then Valentino jumped back in. "A player knows another one. You done did some pimpin'. You brothas have me mixed up with somebody else."

The guards found a knife in his cell so they locked him. I was down to his cell talking to him about the dangers of being in here. The new brothers are the most vulnerable to attacks. They lure then up to the bars and stick them.

Valentino was a real dam character. He went on for about two weeks with all his titles in the world."

Some of the brothas wanted to bust him in his mouth. They had to remember back when we first hit the joint; all the shit we talked about. They had to allow him some room and time to grow like we did. It didn't happen over night.

The first book we gave him to read was *Message to the Black Man,* and then *Great Men of Color*. For two weeks he got real quiet in his cell and one day he stepped in front of my cell with his perm shaved off. The first words that he expressed were remorse for living like a heathen. It hit him and impacted him the same way it hit me. I had felt like I betrayed my people. I knew when they shipped us out he and the others would carry the torch. Valentino told the other brothers he didn't think I had a sense of humor. I'd be funny when I got out. I knew all that talk was a distraction Sometimes you needed it.

CHAPTER 10
SAN QUENTIN

TIRED OF YOU

After being housed downstairs for six months, the guard walked by my cell and told me to roll it up. "You're leaving." About 7 p.m. I rolled my stuff up and one by one we were strip-searched, chained up and put on the Grey Goose.

One of the white dudes tripped on his chains and the guards pushed him down and jumped him. Technically this skinhead was my enemy but in a situation like that we set aside differences and will fight these dogs. They would have had to beat all our asses. The guards saw that we were not budging; we meant what we said. They stopped the foolishness. We had nothing to lose. I looked at the back of the bus. I saw Carl, his dad, and grandfather—three generation of men in their family locked away at one time for pimping.

About 11: 30 p.m. we arrived at San Quentin, an ancient castle by the sea. It looks like a Spanish mission on the inside. One bridge connects it with the rest of the world. San Quentin the last house on the left, the loneliest house on the block, heart break hotel.

The fat guard stepped on the bus and said, "All right, Dorothy. Click your heels three times because you're home." We were taken off the bus and escorted right to the lockup unit. Some of the men there were legends in the prison system. We were rookies just warming up compared to them. Some of the brothas there had been locked up here ten, fifteen, twenty years in lockup and had been soldiers through it all. They were there when there were no laws to protect their rights. Guards could lock you away for in the isolation cell and no one would know, cut off all communication from the outside. They didn't have a problem hanging you, starving you, allowing other prisoner to attack you while you are handcuffed, gun you down.

We were two different generations of men trying to reach out to each other. They had a lot they wanted to share with us, teach us that they wanted us to hear. We wanted them to hear us, too. We had no idea that what we started would reach the magnitude that it reached and beyond. We were a bunch of 14 and 15 year old kids when we started what became known as banging.

Mr. George Jackson was our earthly inspiration in there. He left behind words and actions that inspired men and women locked down all over this country. He was starting to touch the world outside when his life was taken from him. He touched that generation, and the next generation touched us. The whole time I've been down I was surrounded by strong positive brothas, like: Ifoma, Tim J. from Pacoima, Diallo, Chaka, Zoom, Mr. Beak, L.P., Keg, Sule, Ajene, Jihad, Jaha, Mu, Sanyika, mjumbe, Zaki, Imani, Jelani, Zintani.

DIFFERENT

The brothas in the Q. had their own language it was the first time I had ever heard anybody being called a tiddy head motha-fucka or a panny neck motha—fucka.I had never been around brothas like those there in the lockup unit in San Quentin. Willing and ready to die for their own, the brothas there were the most feared group in lockdown any where by the guards. Tears formed up in their eyes when they heard gunshots coming from other parts us the prison, when they thought the brothas were being gunned down. One brotha heard the shots go off on the yard and started climbing the gate on our yard and was shot down. He was going to help the other brothas. The brothas that came before us left a road map, set the standard, set the example. The system locked them down because of the impact they would have on the African American population and other men everywhere. It would have been overwhelming. It would have been a different ballgame for this generation. What made our generation strong was the unity and heart. When we arrived we brought fire to add to the fire. Yet and still they were the baddest motha—fuckas I ever met, the elders.

JEFF

This white dude named Jeff from Carson put hisself in a real messed up position when Ferocious and the others moved on/hit the haters. Jeff got tagged, too. He got cut up pretty bad. He let them idiots inside his head, even though he didn't believe in everything they believed in. He became part of a group discount package because of association. On the yard in the lock unit, the white boys on this yard used to pick on and talk down to Jeff. A couple of times the intense arguments almost turned into fights. They knew Jeff's heart wasn't into it and made arrangements to cut him up.

The white dude next to me is cutting out a knife, and the dude next to JR is cutting out a flat, too. The whole time Jeff and I have been here, we have been dropping each other kites talking about the Lakers, the Dodgers. I dropped Jeff a kite and told him they are cutting out knives. I said I thought they were planning on hitting him. He agreed. He was kind of green when it came to this shit.

I told him to pretend he was real sick and to stay in from the yard for a few days, to cut out a knife, and get off first. Jeff came to the yard a week later, strapped, nervous but ready.

This white dude I call Snake came out on the yard all fired up. He stood around for a moment and then headed straight for the shitter. His knife must have been so far up his ass he had to go to the toilet and shit it out.

I looked at Jeff and said, "Go get that bastard. That's the bastard these other fools get their instructions from. When he pulls that knife out of his ass, that's your ass. Get him."

Jeff jogged one lap around the yard, and he attacks Snake while he is on the shitter and lights his ass up. He didn't expect that. The other white dudes in on the hit weren't paying attention. They heard the commotion, turned around, and made a mad dash toward Jeff. The guards sprayed the yard I was proud of him. You fuckin' stud, Jeff.

THE YOUNGSTERS

The brothers had gotten lit up a few times, lit up bad, coming in all stitched up, complaining. Out there listening to and confused by cowards and fools on the line, they fell into that same complacency of division and got tagged. This generation and the ones that came behind us were not like us, nothing like us. We were beasts when it came to this shit; we never lost. The prison world is a savage cold blooded world where those who expect to live in peace or get caught sleeping pay a price for it. They are not playing up there; they will hit you in chow hall, the yard, shop,

or school or come in the hospital while you are laying up recovering from surgery and finish you off. Age wasn't a factor. In some cases they would attack you while you are hand cuffed or cuffed to something, fuckin cowards.
; any damn thing went on there.

If you were looking for a fair one from the enemy, that wasn't gonna happen; that was not how they fought.You have to understand we are to fuckin big and strong to handle one on one. Those kids had a lot to learn; they didn't understand what they were signing up for when they received that twenty-five or fifty-year term. They stepped off one battlefield and onto a worse one. But what we knew or had learned over the years; there was always gonna be a group of brothers that would rise up.

Roy & Angel

When Roy and Angel hit the streets they wrote me immediately and let me know they were out. They let me know they hooked up with BB for a minute to get established. Three weeks later I received both of their obituaries in the mail. I was devastated. I stayed in my cell for about a week; I didn't want to be bothered. That same year we lost Duck, Ghost, Diamond, Big Duty, and Mad Mark.

The streets ain't nothing to play with.

THE

They are what I am, and I am what they are. We bow down to a different God at night and in the morning our tattoos tell different stories Both proud of what we should be ashamed of. They bring the worst out in me, and I in them. Theoretically and mathematically we increase to meet the need. It comes from what we have and what we are. There is no middle; there is no in-between. Either you are or you aren't. Everything has a concept and a core. Everyone is a soldier for what they believe in

In prison, we are all niggas: black ones, red ones, brown ones, white ones, yellow ones. All niggas fighting for the bottom. You have to be careful that you don't go off on the deep end in a philosophy, a doctrine you can get lost and never come back. Between truth and reality there is a place called balance and common sense. In the grip of pride everything you do and say is right All of these things accumulate and become the enemy.

SANITY

Sometimes you have bad days; sometimes you have bad moments.

Sometimes it is centered on family concerns or your hate for this place, and you have to catch yourself. Every once in a while you go through a phase when you get so tired of being here you don't know what the fuck to do. It is like being up a brick wall; you burn out. All the stroking won't do it, and television, radio, exercise, studying, or reading won't cut it. All relief efforts have been exhausted. The battle now is for the mind. I never had to use my creativity and imagination so much to get over a mountain. Deacon Joe's words would come back to remembrance when it got like this. He would say the devil wants your life and you must fight him in the area of the spirit.

This one particular day the guards wanted to search my cell and I didn't feel like stripping or having my cell searched. I told them I'm not gonna do it. They told me the consequences. I guess we just would have to fight. They came back in riot gear; that back slot opened, and the guards shot the stun gun, then the gas, then the stun and more gas and they asked me to surrender. I'm not gonna put my hands up and surrender.

Never! They shot the stun gun and more gas. It looks like a damn cloud in my cell, and then they racked my cell door and ran in on me. I was gonna get as many of them as I could before they overtook me. It took a lot of them to get the cuffs on me. They took me to a holding tank and told me to strip down. I told them I was not gonna do it; to get ready for round fuckin' two.

The sergeant said, "Just put his ass in a fuckin' cell. I'm tired of his fuckin ass."

One hour later here came Jespah. The guards got him, too. Jespah looked at me and said, "Another fine fuckin' mess you done got me into."

I did ten days in isolation and went back to my cell.

Our Parents

Our mothers follow us from institution to institution, regardless of the crime and no matter how far, no matter how long we are gone, rain or shine, jail term after jail term. My mother traveled in the snow once to see me. That is what love is and what love does. Our parents beat themselves up and blamed themselves to some degree for our failures and disappointments. Parents say, "I should have done this and done that."

Most parents from our generation did what they could do and all they knew how. The environment plays a part, and then you inherit stuff and there are some things that are just in you. I owe my mother an apology for my behavior.

CHAPTER 11
THE WALL

VISITS

Today I received a surprise visit from my mother and my brothers. I haven't seen them in about seven years. I didn't know what to say. The tears in her eyes made me want to cry. I see the effects of what I have done has done to her, and I am sorry. I should have been a better son. She traveled 600 miles to visit me behind glass for 30 minutes. Saying good-bye is never easy; seeing them did me a lot of good.

Some of the men here don't have family. They were raised in the foster care system. Some of the men come from broken, divided families where there was a lot going on in the home, such as addictions. Some of the men parents have passed on. Some of the men never had caring parents. Some of the men here had it all and ran off every one that ever loved them. Some of the men never get mail or visits. Family makes all the difference in the world. I left a little brother behind that looked up to me, and I let him down.

GUARDS

Some of the guards in prison just come to work and put in their eight to twelve hours and go home. It is just a job; they try not to ruffle any feathers. If you ask them to do something for you, as long as it was within the guidelines of the rules, they would do it for you. Some of the guards understand that you should treat people and talk to them like you would like to be treated and talked to. Most of the time, you would get a positive response. It cuts down on some of the friction between guards and prisoners. You don't mess with me, and I won't fuck with you. I don't want to play with you; don't play with me. It's not always the guards; sometimes it's the prisoners some of the men there had problems.

Most of the female guards stay their distance from the prisoners. There are a few that feel they have something to prove, that they ain't no punk. They have chest out and gloves on ready to go; they like to get in there and mix it up.

Then there are the other ones who like to keep shit going, setting up prisoners to get hit and lie. They have their hands in a lot of shit,dirty. They come to work and try to take out on you the things that are going wrong in their homes. They talk crazy to you, mess with your food, mess with your mail, and shortstop paperwork.

Some of the guards here don't like African Americans. You can hear it in the smart shit that comes from their mouths and attitudes toward us. Don't let them be in the gun tower when something jumps off.

THE SYSTEM

The California prison system underwent some radical changes in the 1980s. There was shifting of power, new alignments, experiments, putting the old on the back burner, moving people around. The opening up of many new facilities, no more bars, cameras everywhere. New sentencing laws and guidelines for sentencing. A new system for categorizing prisoners. The prison system went from being prisons to concentration camps. Then the prison system had to prepare for the influx of other ethnic groups: Eastern Europeans, Chinese, Armenians, Russians, Jamaicans, and the Latinos.

I had just stepped on the yard, and I saw a pair of eyes on me from the Hispanic yard, watching me like a hawk. He was staring at me like he knew me. Everywhere I went, his eyes were on me. So I came to the gate to stare back, and he was just smiling and said, "You don't know nobody. Know more, Johnny."

Then I looked real close and deep, and I said, "That's Li'l Bobby." I was in shock. This was his second trip to the joint. We couldn't talk to each other the way we really wanted to, because of politics. He took down my information and said he would write to me through his sister.

A week later, I got a letter from Bobby, and he told me about the last fifteen years and who he has run into in the prison system. The last time I saw Bobby he turned out this high school and a few drug runs. Bobby was in front of this school with his low rider and was talking to this white girl and some jealous white dudes jumped on him, and Wino told them bean town was that way. Bobby rode over to the projects and got us. We went in four cars. The Mexicans were in three cars, but shit, it must have been about twenty of them in each car. We had the bud; they had the brew. After a serious head tightening session, it was time to ride. We flipped the whole school upside down.

Bobby went home a year later. Just before his birthday, I got his obituary in the mail. He got killed over a dispute behind his sister. That was my friend, my brown brother since the second grade. Man, I miss him.

CAT & DOGS

The men we used to fight with like cats and dogs years ago when we were all locked down together. They were still there also

As we got older our relationships with each other were slightly different. For some of the men, there was still some animosity there. We showed each other a certain amount of respect.

Some of us talked to each other when the opportunity presented itself. We go back a long way in the system.

The guards were playing with our food so Jespah threw his dinner tray on the guards.The guards come back on our tier in riot gear and attack Jespah and remove him from his cell. The brothas and I got upset and the sergeant that ordered the attack we hit his ass with piss and shit. while the sergeant was running trying to get out of the way of the piss and shit he stepped in front of my cell.

I reached through the bars and I popped him in the back with my state shoe.He jumped in the air and hollered son of a bitch.Go get that bastard they were still in riot gear they stepped in front of my cell they didn't ask me shit.Even though I would have said no, they are suspose to ask if would like to surrender. You won't time to prepare fore the tear gas.They shoot gas, the stun gun then they run in on me. It is to many of them but I am gonna snatch their gas mask off and make them breathe this shit to.Once I am hand cuffed they take me to an isolated part of the jail the sergeant hits me with a few body shots. and he sprays maise in my face. I tell him you hit like a bitch. I am taken down stairs to the isolation cells placed right next to Casper the nigga hater.For ten days Casper and I talk about the lakers, dodgers,women, our parents.I saw through his tattoos and the anger and I know for the first time he began to understand me. I don't dislike people because of the color of their skin.For ten days it was like there was nothing between us two men just talking.Because of politics he will not be allowed to speak to me once we go back up stairs. We don't impose the bull shit on our people.We talk when the opportunity presents itself.He thinks he knows more about sports than I do. What I respect about him is I never saw him run or back down from anybody.

Twisted

We used to be the kind of people that would look after and take care of each other. These youngsters from the generation behind us got away from that. If it was up to some of the brothers, they would run the place like a pirate ship, run it like the streets, all about that dollar, stepping over one another.

The weak would have to pay rent to live here, pay to eat or get that tray snatched, pay to use the phones, extort brothers out of their canteen, and have other men write home to their families to send money to keep the thugs off of them. It was just how fucked up some of our people were. I say put a hole in them.

Some of the weak would rather switch and make monthly payments than fight back.

If there weren't any brothers here to stand up for the weak, the weak would be in trouble. If they were really that damn bad, they wouldn't be on the line programming.

THE CRIPS

In my gang-banging days, I was a well-known member of the Bounty Hunters gang. I traveled from institution to institution with the Crips. I have to say it there were some bad boys that came from the Crips, strong and courageous brothas that hit the prison system in the 1970s. I have nothing but big respect for them. Some of them had big names; some of them didn't. They know who they are. The Crips and ex-Crips made up the majority of our warriors. They always showed up for the big dance and put their life on the line to come to the aid of other brothers under attack and did what they had to do.

We formed a bond that would never be broken my brothers forever: Pit Bull, Black Johnny, Sugar Bear, Michael Johnson, Sule, Ajene, Ice, Jomo from Aliso, Bosco, Big Boobie from Grande, Bam, Bad Habit, Baby D, Jackal, Ant, Rabbit, Dinosaur, Dillenger, Pretty Pretty Mike or Michael C., Jack Rabbit, Yogi, Mad Hoover, Mousie, L'il Bunchie, El. Jr., Dead Eye, Wayne D. Eddie and Mid and Raymond Washington, Hoover Joe, Tony S. and Beamon and miller that was in Fenner with me. The brothers from the Palladium incident were the first of our kind to enter the prison system; they had to stand with the weight of this whole gang situation on their shoulders.

The brothers that stood out from the blood gangs: CC & MM from the Bishops; Frog and Blade, D. Eley, M. Ford, Green Eyes, Harold Glen, Cabala, DB, Bernard H., from the Bounty Hunters; R. Frazier and Lug, Dadisi, Diallo, TD from the Piru; Roe and Smitty from the AV. Brims; and Biggie Rat from the A.P.B.s and from the Swans JC. My way of saying I appreciated them and what they stood for.

Many things have happened over the years but I remember what they were. Brothers also special to me are Tim J. from Pacoima; and L.P., Tark, G.P, Zoom, Ifoma, Keg, Big Duty, Big Dookie, Imani, Jelani, Jaha, Mjumbe, Mu, Pee-Wee,Chaka, Flan, Sanyika.from Frisco,n R. Beak, Jespah from the LBC; Grant, CB, Cleve, Zintani,. Brothers close to my heart and special. We were really a special unique, strong, dominant generation. There has never been a generation like us. Brothas that left us to soon: Khatari, Tyrone, Natural, Michael Johnson, Pit bull and Big James Miller, Tookie

The problems, that the more militant brothers had with the bangers was there was a war going on at the time. They felt that the bangers—especially the big name ones—should have been the first ones on the front line with a knife in their hands. Instead of promoting banging and keeping the grudges going, the first blood gang to hit the prison system hard was the Bounty Hunters.

The one Crip that was the closest to me was Big Boobie from Grande; we met in camp. I had been in places where I was the only person from a blood gang there. Some bloods were scared to say where they were from. There were times when I was outnumbered 50 to 1 by the Crips; another time 80 to 1 in the jail system. I was ready to fight. I just didn't know I had to fight everybody at the same time. I have to say it if were not for Boobie and who he was and his influence, they probably would have all attacked me. L'il Bunchie, Bam, Pit Bull, Michael Johnson from Harlem godfathers also went out of their way for me to keep shit down. I was high on some of their priority lists.

My Story

With the exception of the retarded stuff, my story is the same as most of the young that have ever entered or still enter the prison system: our backgrounds, the anger, where we missed it, the rebellion, and the failures.

In this punishment and somewhere in the correction in the system, you get lost and devoured by it.

, I can't quite describe or explain what being in prison does to you. You loose some of you the part that you need.

I knew when I wrote this book, not everybody was gonna understand.

The prison world is a different world with its own set of rules and regulations, politics, and hate. It is the perfect breeding ground for anger, failure, and disappointment to grow.

You come to prison with a few issues and leave with a whole new set of problems.

You try to repair some of the broken pieces,

It takes you awhile to become who you are

I wasn't always like the kid the man in the book.I went to school every day led my elementary school to baseball championships, two time jr. Olympic track and field champ in the 400, kick,punt, pass champ. Good enough to play pro baseball But I found something in the streets that found a way into my head and my heart and held on I started off doing little things like lying to my mother and ditching school.Then stealing cars, fighting and it worked it's way up to gangs and guns and making them back door drug runs

STRIPPED DOWN

They strip you of everything you have, and they do it layer by layer. You won't even feel or see it. You won't see it in yourself, but you will see it in others. They will take who you are from it, if you let them.

The only things they couldn't take or touch were our memories. On oldie but goody night in D.V.I., the music would take me back to a certain place and time, before all of the confusion, bangin', and to a time period when all of my friends were still alive. Certain songs would put me back at the 112th Street School, Markham, the W.L.C.A.C., high school, and with my family. When it was oldies night, I would go back for a few hours or the length of the show and in my mind I went to that place in time.

Some of the men in prison got all into it. They yelled, screamed, shouted, and danced in their cells. They had a ball on oldies night. Some of the men said it was the best time to write letters.

I couldn't hang out like that all of the time. Back in 1973 it wasn't healthy. You would lose a sense of reality.

One time one of my homeboys from Watts and I were in isolation cells. They said I had cut off part of my bed to make a weapon. They pulled him off of the line on some bullshit hearsay. He knew I was in there but didn't recognize me because he hadn't seen me since Markham.

He had never been in an isolation cell with nothing in it, and it was getting to him. The walls were closing in on him. That shit wasn't nothing to me. I was gonna sing and do push-ups for ten days. He was talking crazy, so I had to get his attention before he snapped. I called over to him. I began to talk to him about Markham Junior High, Jordan. For ten days, from A to Z, we talked about every classmate we could remember, all the pretty girls, the girls that used to make us laugh in class, the brothers that stood out, the bullies, the brothers that were fun to be around. We talked about the teachers and the staff. By the fifth day, he was pulling through it. I also showed him how to play chess.

At the end of his ten days, he went back on the line or into general population. I was going to be back upstairs to finish my prison term in lock-up. It was good to talk to somebody from home. Since I have been gone

Bad news finds you no matter where you are and it saddens you.Some of the homeboys I'm really gonna miss passed away they were genuine and fun to be around rest in peace: Andre and Michael Cooper, Ray Hawthorne, Tony and Rhea Boyce, Boo—Boo, Blue, Benny Beaver, Derrick Pounds, Slow Drag, Peter wallace.and one of the twins.

And the home girls : Cheryl Madison, Betty Williams, Erie Pickens, Marilyn Brister,Charolette Sheppard, Gail Brown, Janet Johnson and my cousins Jimmy Will and Larry, kilroy, Will.

FULL OF FIRE

When you are young and full of fire, there is a feeling of greatness. You feel untouchable. The longer you get away with your shit, the stronger that feeling becomes. Nobody can tell you shit, and your system is fool proof.

Everyone in prison thought that same damn thing. That's why we were there. There is no exception to the rule. There is always a slip-up point or you trap yourself, and then there are the deal makers and deal grabbers. There are too many things working against you that are designed to put you in prison.

Ain't nothing great or glorious about being in prison. It is a fucking nightmare. Stripped of everything and locked away from everyone that you love and from everyone who

170

loves you. You are on constant lockdown twenty-three hours a day; people tell you what to eat, when to go to bed; no women, no future. It is not where you want to be.

It ain't what you think it is. You really need to think before you pick up a damn gun. The consequences are a lot harder to deal with than you think. The young men coming into the system don't realize what they have lost yet. For a while they will use all of the excuses to justify what they did. After some years roll by, they realize that they're standing by themselves. Their eyes open, and they realize that what they have done cost them their life. They begin to see this gang stuff in a whole different light.

Don't throw your life away. Life is to short to be spending it behind bars. I hope you hear this so you wont be sitting inside of a cell waiting to get out.

Never get tired of doing the right thing.

There is so much to live for and to do

The dead and the dying live here . . .

CONSEQUENCES

Time and reality change you
You do things you regret. You do things you will always regret.
One day it hits you. You wake up.
You see your dreams disappear
The girl of your dreams marries someone else
The peak years of your life pass you by
Your family members began to pass away
Friends and teachers pass away
You have been gone so long, friends and classmates have forgotten about you.
You don't get a chance to see your children grow, and they grow up resenting you for it.
And you sit in your cell, and you sit in your cell and you sit in your cell
And you age slowly.

End

CPSIA information can be obtained at www.ICGtesting.com
Printed in the USA
BVOW071349091012

302555BV00002B/124/P